# Dedication

For two who left far too soon:

In loving memory of my dear father, Leonard Gross, and my teacher and cherished friend, Norman Kaner.

# STAYING CENTERED

## CURRICULUM LEADERSHIP IN A TURBULENT ERA

### STEVEN J. GROSS

ASSOCIATION FOR SUPERVISION AND CURRICULUM DEVELOPMENT

ALEXANDRIA, VIRGINIA USA

Association for Supervision and Curriculum Development
1250 N. Pitt Street • Alexandria, Virginia 22314-1453 USA
Telephone: 1-800-933-2723 or 703-549-9110 • Fax: 703-299-8631
Web site: http://www.ascd.org • E-mail: member@ascd.org

Gene R. Carter, *Executive Director*
Michelle Terry, *Assistant Executive Director,*
*Program Development*
Nancy Modrak, *Director, Publishing*
John O'Neil, *Acquisitions Editor*
Julie Houtz, *Managing Editor of Books*
Kathie Felix, *Associate Editor*
Kathleen Larson Florio, *Copy Editor*
Deborah Whitley, *Proofreader*

Charles D. Halverson, *Project Assistant*
Gary Bloom, Director, *Editorial, Design,*
*and Production Services*
Karen Monaco, *Senior Designer*
Tracey A. Smith, *Production Manager*
Dina Murray, *Production Coordinator*
John Franklin, *Production Coordinator*
Valerie Sprague, *Desktop Publisher*

The publishers have generously given permission to use quotations from the following copyrighted works. From *On the Pulse of Morning*, by Maya Angelou. Copyright 1993 by Maya Angelou. Reprinted by permission of Random House, Inc. From *Tomorrow Is Now*, by Eleanor Roosevelt. Copyright 1963 by The Estate of Anna Eleanor Roosevelt. Copyright renewed 1991. Reprinted by permission of HarperCollins Publishers, Inc.

ASCD publications present a variety of viewpoints. The views expressed or implied in this book should not be interpreted as official positions of the Association.

Printed in the United States of America.

February 1998 member book (p). ASCD Premium, Comprehensive, and Regular members periodically receive ASCD books as part of their membership benefits. No. FY98-5.

ASCD Stock No.: 198008     ASCD member price: $15.95     nonmember price: $18.95

**Library of Congress Cataloging-in-Publication Data**
Gross, Steven J.
    Staying centered : curriculum leadership in a turbulent era /
Steven J. Gross
        p.   cm.
    Includes bibliographical references (p.    ).
    ISBN 0-87120-292-1 (pbk.)
        1. Curriculum planning—United States—Case studies.
    2. Education—United States—Curricula—Case studies.
    3. Educational change—United States—Case studies.  4. Curriculum
    planning—Canada—Case studies.  5. Education—Canada—Curricula-
    -Case studies.  6. Educational change—Canada—Case studies.
    I. Association for Supervision and Curriculum Development.
    II. Title.
    LB2806.15.G76    1998
    375'.001—DC21                                          98-4565
                                                              CIP

02  01  00  99  98        5  4  3  2  1

# STAYING CENTERED:

## Curriculum Leadership in a Turbulent Era

# Acknowledgments

Thanking everyone who has made this book possible is a most difficult but important task since I have been given so much help.

First, I want to acknowledge the support and crucial guidance I received from Ron Brandt and the professionals at ASCD who believed that I had a worthwhile idea and stuck with me. I also greatly appreciate the criticism, conceptual thinking, and friendship given to me by my department chair and friend, Steve Garger. The whole Trinity College Community has smiled upon me for the duration of this work and I have received vital financial support from them. My colleague John Duval of Castleton State College helped me greatly with general ideas and specific references. With great gratitude and affection, I wish to thank the principals, superintendents, teachers, students, families, and community members at all 10 school or district sites whose willingness to create and sustain authentic educational change has been an inspiration.

On a personal note, I wish to thank my mother and stepfather, Esther and Herb Barg, my sister Barbara Kutner, my cousin Ken Gross and, most especially, my beloved wife Jean and children Emily and Will. You inspire me every day in the pursuit of a better system of education.

# Introduction

I have worried about the issue of sustainable curriculum development for a long time. As a high school social studies teacher in Philadelphia, I learned that the needs of my students were varied, yet they all had to face the same complex world after graduation. I spent long hours thinking of ways to respond to diverse needs while helping everyone reach high standards. During graduate school I researched school-to-work internships in New York and concluded that more time was needed if excellent programs, which stretched the curriculum offerings of school, were to have a chance to develop. As a curriculum director in rural Vermont, I found that we could make a great deal of progress in upgrading our learning program and the skills of our professionals when we agreed to a serious, long-range plan. When I served as one of two chiefs of curriculum and instruction at the Vermont Department of Education, I saw the same pattern. I was able to coordinate our Common Core of Learning program because we had a high-quality plan developed with the help of many people who were dedicated to listening to thousands of our fellow citizens over an extended period of time.

Yet, over the past half decade, the ability of educators to create plans that can move in steady, logical fashion along clearly determined time lines has all but evaporated. Whether we like it or not, we are living in a turbulent era. Until recently, this was considered a novel situation. Dozens of books, magazine articles, and radio and television shows have been devoted to the topic. Workshops describing the effects of rapid change probably have given rise to many careers. Now the novelty is over; we simply accept the fact that many of the givens we once counted on are gone. Families move so frequently that the concept of community may seem more of a memory than anything else. Trust in institutions such as public schools has too often been replaced with an almost automatic cynicism. Funding for education is not predictable, nor is it sufficient to assure equity. Even the basic relationship between the federal, state, and local levels of government is shifting. One parent of a high school student near Toronto described the situation most accurately: "The world is running like crazy and everyone is running behind it. . . . The way we used to do education and the way education has to be is pulling [in two directions], and the kids are in the middle now."

In this environment, how are educators and the communities they serve going to set a meaningful and relevant learning agenda? How will they show the kind of curriculum leadership that demonstrates solid results over time? What follows is the story of 10 sites in the United States and Canada that are doing just that.

## Using History to Understand the Current Crisis

To prepare for this study, I first reflected on my training in history. Spending time at Harvard University's Gutman Library, I gained needed perspective on the development of today's dilemma. From Stephen Kern's (1986) wonderful book on changing perspectives in culture, time, and space, I learned how difficult it was to create a standard time zone—even within the same city—only 100 years ago! That and other examples made me think about how different we were as a society such a short time ago. Alfred North Whitehead's advice in his essay "The Aims of Education" (1929) had a surprisingly relevant ring, as did the accounts organized by Harold Rugg and the National Society for the Study of Education in their 1926 yearbook entitled *The Foundations and Technique of Curriculum Construction*. Herbert M. Kliebard's excellent study, *The Struggle for the American Curriculum 1893–1958* (1986), described the themes of progressive education, essentialism, existentialism, and perennialism that also play a strong part in today's debates.

Ruminating over this historical backdrop back in Vermont, I found myself wandering across the street from my office at Trinity College to the grave of John Dewey, hoping to get a bit of inspiration. I ended my visit by thinking that our era had many of the same qualities faced by our ancestors a century ago. They too lived through the transition from an older economy to a new one. They had to reconcile themselves to a future that was hard to predict, and they approached the problem with varied, and often conflicting, belief systems. Being a curriculum leader in the 1890s was no easier than being one today. But history taught me something even more important: Thoughtful educators faced their turbulence with vigor a century ago. I started to feel that we could do the same today—if we could learn from some powerful models.

## How This Book Is Organized

This book is based upon visits to 10 sites in the United States and Canada. I chose some after contacting national organizations such as the Coalition of Essential Schools and the University of Georgia's League of Professional Schools. Others were chosen in consultation with government agencies such as the Wisconsin Department of Public Instruction. Still others came through networking with citizen action groups such as Arkansas Friends for Better Schools and Kentucky's Prichard Committee for Academic Excellence. One group, the Heron Institute of Madison, Wisconsin, contacted me over the Internet after I made an appeal for possible sites through ASCD.

Regardless of the origin of the contact, all of the examples have common traits. First, all are public schools or school districts. I decided to focus on public education because public schools face a very different challenge than do independent schools. Public schools must work with students and families who live within a given community. Students may or may not approve of their school's mission; they may not even know that one exists. Therefore, limiting my investigation to public schools seemed a wise way to focus on comparable situations and challenges.

Second, all of these sites have been involved in the process of curriculum leadership for several years. This means that they have seen the process from a start-up phase through early development, and they have lived through an important testing period. They were also successful in their curriculum development efforts, although they demonstrated their success in different ways. Although I was impressed with the quality of these institutions, these very good schools are not my version of North America's top 10 educational sites. That was not my intention, and placing them on a pedestal would be a disservice to the schools and their communities.

Third, in choosing sites, I strove to present a good cross-section of institutions. Geographically speaking, there is one site in New England, one in the Mid-Atlantic, one in the Sun Belt, one in the Far West, one in Canada, two in the Midwest, and three in the South. The sites also vary by level. One is an organization of teachers, four are elementary schools, two are high schools, one is a small K–12 system, and two are comprehensive K–12 districts. In terms of setting, one is in an inner city, two are in rural areas, one is in a densely populated suburb of a major city, and the others are in middle-class suburban neighborhoods. Most have a significant population of students living at or near the poverty level, and five of the sites have a growing minority population. Just as important, the sites have approached curriculum leadership in a richly varied way, demonstrating that there is no one right answer to this problem.

As used in this book, the terms *curriculum leaders* and *curriculum leadership* refer to both individuals and the organizations they are part of, and the activity they are engaged in. The terms refer to active participation in moving schools forward to provide a learning program that is vigorous and relevant in preparing students for a successful future and that demonstrates results over time.

## THE 10 SITES

1. *A.L. Burruss Elementary School* in Marietta, Georgia, is an example of a school that became a curriculum leader by first engaging in instructional change. In Burruss's case, this meant moving toward a new language arts program that combined literature and writing, as well as traditional phonics. Burruss also exemplifies a school where shared governance is taken seriously by administrators, faculty, staff, and students. Burruss has about 550 students.

2. *The Cabot School* is one of the few small-town K–12 school systems left in Vermont. Its small size has not kept Cabot from making some big changes in recent years. Responding to a state competition, the community led an effort to create a standards-driven curriculum designed to greatly improve student performance. Since then, Cabot has been a leader in the Green Mountain State. It has established standards and instructional guidelines, and the faculty is working hard to modify instruction to help all students reach the new targets. Cabot's enrollment is about 250.

3. *Hansberry Elementary School* is located in District 12 in the Bronx, New York City. It joined the Hudson Institute's Modern Red Schoolhouse project in 1993, thus adopting the Core Knowledge curriculum and other major changes. The school's population is about 500.

4. *The Heron Institute* is the creation of teachers in the Madison, Wisconsin, area. Working together with support from grants, these educators hold conferences in science and mathematics, produce publications, and exchange student work. Just as important, they support their own professional development and help one another to create classrooms where student inquiry in all subjects is valued. Because they often work without the institutional support of administrators and regular budgets, their achievements are doubly impressive.

5. *The Northeast Arkansas School District* in Paragould, Arkansas, enrolls 2,800 students from preschool to grade 12. The eight schools in this district have developed scores of local curriculum innovations, ranging from an early childhood education center to a school-to-work program for special education seniors.

6. *Oceana High School* is located just south of San Francisco. Although the school had been in existence for 25 years and was successful in its traditional program, it was reorganized in 1991. Working with the Bay Area Coalition of Essential Schools and with many elements of the community, the school emerged with a restructured plan emphasizing students' responsibility for their learning and the creation of a strong sense of community within and beyond the school. Oceana has about 800 students.

7. *Sinclair Secondary School* is part of the Durham Board of Education just outside of Toronto. This large district includes nearly 60,000 students and more than 5,600 teachers. Sinclair has about 1,200 students. The school was established in 1994, though its origins may be traced back over several years since key leaders came from other schools in the same district. School leaders and their community enjoyed a wonderful degree of freedom to experiment with interdisciplinary curriculum in the 9th grade. Their affiliation with the University of Toronto's Learning Consortium greatly aided their efforts.

8. *Squires Elementary School* in Lexington, Kentucky, exemplifies how a school can integrate a strong statewide reform movement with its own ideas about curriculum leadership. Squires complies with the state's Learning Goals and Academic Expectations but has adopted the Different Ways of Knowing curriculum designed by the Galef Institute in Los Angeles. This program promotes an interdisciplinary approach to social studies and history and includes a strong dose of faculty development and student-directed learning. A look at Squires also provides some insights into the workings of the Kentucky Education Reform Act. Squires has about 500 students.

9. *Three Oaks Elementary School* near Fort Myers, Florida, made history by becoming the first school in the United States to adopt E.D. Hirsch's Core Knowledge curriculum. This required many of the accomplished staff in this school of about 1,000 students to increase their own content knowledge, as well as find novel ways to deliver this new curricular approach. Teachers' close working relationships and their detailed cooperative plans are particularly impressive.

10. *The Verona Area School District* is located just outside of Madison, Wisconsin. This K–12 district has 3,600 students in seven buildings. Over the past several years Verona has undertaken serious efforts at strategic planning, with special emphasis on a new district mission. To progress further, however, Verona had to deal with a serious division in its community over the direction of that mission.

Although the facts that describe these sites stand out, specific images of my time with the remarkable people who are part of them remain just as fresh. In Madison, Wisconsin, I remember sitting in Mark Wagler's home late one snowy afternoon while a half dozen

Heron Institute teachers lit the room with stories of children learning how to approach science as a scientist might. In Paragould, Arkansas, I was privileged to spend time with Tommy Johnson and his high school students as they explained how they monitored water quality in their aquaculture project. They raised enough fish in one year to feed 300 guests. In Pacifica, California, I listened in admiration as Oceana's principal, Lois Jones, joined with parents, teachers, and students to tell me how a community had banded together to save a school whose mission and curriculum they believed in. In the Bronx, Hansberry 2nd graders taught me how to classify pebbles, rocks, and sand in Spanish and in English. In Marietta, Georgia, newly elected student council officers at Burruss Elementary School reflected on the difficulty and importance of participatory government.

Altogether, I conducted more than 140 interviews with more than 250 people. In almost every case, I was able to spend considerable time in classes to see how curriculum changes affected the lives of children. Parents and community members helped greatly to round out the picture of their school. I also benefited from many school, district, state, and university documents.

### Four Chapters Focusing on Four Questions

When trying to decide how to organize this book, I considered presenting a series of case studies, perhaps loosely organized around common themes. However, after reflection and conversations with teachers and administrators, I decided to create an integrated account that used the lessons learned at the sites to help solve four essential problems faced by those who wish to become curriculum leaders. These problems—each corresponding to a chapter in the book—can be stated as four major questions, each containing a series of related questions:

- *How did these institutions start the process of curriculum leadership in the first place?* What preconditions do schools or districts need before they start? What qualities do school leaders need? What must be understood about the relationship among curriculum, instruction, and assessment before starting? What different routes might schools take when they start to become curriculum leaders?

- *What successful curriculum plans have these schools and districts used?* What are the main ways these schools and districts have conducted their curriculum work? What do the plans emphasize and how do they relate to district and state mandates? How have these schools and districts created a balance between interdisciplinary and discipline-specific learning? What underlying philosophies guide these curriculum plans and how might they blend together?

- *How do these sites sustain development over time?* How do they invent and implement curriculum change at the same time? What key activities do administrators undertake to sustain a positive climate, establish important supporting structures, and help with the inevitable transitions? What qualities do teachers have that make them effective in these schools? What professional standards do they maintain? How do teacher teams operate? How do teachers participate in shared governance to direct their schools? How are communities organized to support curriculum leadership? When and how do they act as initiators of change? How do they act as strategic problem solvers? When do they engage in hands-on instruction?

- *How have these schools and districts survived turbulence and become stronger because of it?* What levels of turbulence are there? How do educators know which one is occurring at a particular time? What's the best response to each kind of turbulence?

Each chapter ends with some questions that I hope will help you connect this study to your own situation. You will find these under the heading "Consider for a Moment."

My hope is that this book will be useful no matter what your role. If you are a school or district administrator, the information may help you organize your staff and families as you approach curriculum leadership. If you are a teacher, you can learn how colleagues around the country work with administrators and families to change their schools into exciting places for students. You may find a way to get such changes started in your school. If you are a parent or a school board member, you may find ways to help initiate changes with other policymakers. I also have constructed the book to be of use to readers who are at different stages of the process—from preparing to start on the road, through the first school year, and up to the time when turbulence becomes an uncomfortable reality.

Perhaps the most moving thing I learned from all of the hours spent conducting research, transcribing notes, reading documents, and reflecting on the emerging picture is that curriculum leadership is highly possible even in these turbulent times. I think an examination of the details will support that conclusion.

# Getting Started

The horizon leans forward,
Offering you space
To place new steps of change
—FROM "ON THE PULSE OF MORNING," MAYA ANGELOU, 1993

Like any complex activity, curriculum leadership can seem overwhelming. Even if a school or district wants to take greater responsibility for the learning agenda, how can they best begin? One helpful idea is to consider the many available guides that offer general principles and steps to take. As important as these directions are, however, it is essential to understand how they operate in context. In the real world, how does curriculum leadership originate and sustain itself, especially at the early stages? What preconditions need to be in place before curriculum leadership takes off? What kind of leaders seem to be successful in guiding curriculum innovation? How does local curriculum development relate to assessment and instruction, and how can leaders use this knowledge to set their course? What approaches to curriculum leadership might schools and districts take? What roles can the community take in the early stages?

## Setting a Foundation:
## Four Preconditions for Curriculum Leadership

All of the sites described in this book had created what might be called preconditions for curriculum leadership. Thinking of the hierarchy devised by Abraham Maslow (1954), it would be difficult to ask a school or district to become self-actualized if basic issues such as safety were not taken care of. Curriculum leadership is not meant to fix a broken system. It is meant to respond to the demands of the future. Establishing an innovative agenda for learning assumes other structures exist. It is the basic stability of these settings that seems to permit enlightened experimentation. Likewise, the ballast provided by these basics helps the schools and districts survive even severe turbulence. As one board member told me, "It was the basic strength of the district which pulled us through." Here are some of the stabilizing characteristics that these sites had before they started down the road of curricular leadership:

- Success according to traditional definitions
- Safety, attendance, and building maintenance well in hand
- Good communication between site and community
- Team spirit

*Success according to traditional definitions.* For some this meant leading or being near the top in their area in standardized test scores. For others, this meant having a high percentage of students going on to further study after high school. Whatever the measure, these schools had seen success but had grown impatient with the limits of success as traditionally defined. To paraphrase one principal's remarks, "Sure we were teaching a lot of information and students seemed to be learning, but we were afraid that our standards were not high enough." Or, as an Oceana administrator described things before the school's transformation, "Our school was successful in some ways, for some students, by some measures; dropout rates were low, an average of 75 percent of the graduates attended college, and there was a strong honors program. However, we were not meeting the needs of enough students to prepare them for work and life in the next century."

*Safety, attendance, and building maintenance well in hand.* These sites did not expect curriculum leadership to solve school violence problems; nor did they expect it to bring students to school, although they did use it as a way to increase motivation. The buildings themselves were in good condition before plans were laid for a new learning agenda. In fact, 7 of the 10 sites occupied buildings less than 10 years old.

*Good communication between site and community.* Families were comfortable coming to the schools and were familiar with school and district leaders as well as faculty. Some sites had strong support groups—such as parent-teacher organizations—that were welcomed in the school and played a part in the school's inner workings.

*Team spirit.* Teachers were respected as hard workers and high achievers. Administrators were well regarded and engaged in creative projects. Some sites had long histories of leadership before they took off for even higher places. The Cabot School had hosted a small-schools conference for educators in New England for many years before they began to set a whole new path for themselves.

These characteristics suggest that places with stable environments where learning is occurring and where morale is high in and beyond the school are places likely to push to the next higher level of development. These schools and districts had done the background exercising that makes the marathon run of curriculum leadership possible. When leaders ask, "All right, we know that we are doing well, but isn't there something more for us to try?" they are ready to take up the challenge.

## 10 Qualities of Curriculum Leaders

The significance of effective leadership is a continuing theme in our society. Students of European history read such classics as Machiavelli's *The Prince*, business school classes analyze successful models of corporate leadership in great detail, and popular historians such as Doris Kearns Goodwin describe the personal and public lives of such leaders as Franklin and Eleanor Roosevelt in best-selling books.

The need for sound leadership in our schools also has drawn

much attention, especially in recent years. Leithwood (1992) has written about transformational leaders who are capable of inspiring serious organizational change. In the introduction to *The Work of Restructuring Schools*, Ann Lieberman (1995) illustrates the care two principals took to bring teachers along in a gradual process of change. Others tell us that we need leaders who can create effective shared governance if teachers can ever be expected to own change in their schools. Although the roles and tasks of leaders appear to evolve, the need for energetic, thoughtful, and strategic people to lead organizations remains constant.

Along with the preconditions described earlier, the schools and districts in this group had dynamic site leadership—usually an admired principal or superintendent. The importance of such a person is hard to overstate. One influential board member in Cabot, Vermont, explained the role this way: "Leadership is not just a vision, but [also] skill in helping people get where they want to go."

Looking back, it is hard to imagine these schools without that kind of person at their helm. Yet, these leaders came from no single mold. Some served as building principals; others were superintendents of school districts; one was a classroom teacher. Some were occupying a formal leadership position for the first time; others had many years of experience. Some were in mid-career; others told me that this would probably be their last assignment before retirement. They all were revered by the faculty, community members, and students.

With all of this variety, what traits did they have in common? Here are 10 qualities all of the leaders shared:

- Experienced but still growing
- Centered on students and families
- Willing to experiment but not reckless
- Highly engaged but not overwhelmed
- Trusting but not naive
- Powerful but not overbearing
- Visible but quiet
- Dignified but informal
- Demanding but understanding

• Highly ambitious—but for their group, not themselves

Chapter 3 describes how these qualities play out in the daily life of the sites. Here is a brief elaboration of each one.

*Experienced but still growing.* The leaders typically had 15 to 20 years of experience, in some cases all in the classroom. They had a remarkable degree of knowledge about their setting. For example, Lee Vent, superintendent of schools in the Northeast Arkansas School District, described in detail the cultures and histories of the major sections of Arkansas, showing his understanding of the area. Most of the leaders had been known and trusted community members for many years. Yet they saw themselves as evolving and growing. As leaders such as Lois Jones of Oceana High School described what they were discovering, their eyes literally lit up with enthusiasm.

*Centered on students and families.* Clearly the entire focus of these enterprises and their leaders was on learners. Marge Sable of the Cabot School used the improvement of learning as the one test by which everything was measured—even when deciding what paper to buy for 1st grade classes. These leaders stated this priority, but more importantly, they lived it. Even highly attractive innovations such as interdisciplinary courses had to pass this test.

*Willing to experiment but not reckless.* Montrose Spencer, principal of Hansberry Elementary School, showed this characteristic of flexible invention when she described how the school combined phonics with whole language to create a blended approach to literacy. Sometimes the leader had to be convinced, as when students at one elementary school wanted to start a student council. The leader had established a system to try out new ideas and gave that one a chance. One year later, he spoke about it with pride. The leaders were also highly strategic. One principal wanted to increase foreign language instruction. She realized that if she suggested that all 9th grade students take French, parents might criticize the plan for being too demanding for some. If she said, however, that all 4th grade students needed to be introduced to French, families might feel more comfortable, and, in time, that would lead to all 9th grade students taking French.

*Highly engaged but not overwhelmed.* One leader described the goal as taking the work but not herself seriously. This is easy to say but, for many, difficult to do, especially in a busy building. These people dealt with the same kinds of emergencies as anyone in similar jobs. Conferences with unhappy families, emergency meetings at the district office, intervention between fighting students, cheering up a faculty member, even dealing with the possible closing of the school all happened during my visits. What distinguished these cases from others was that the leaders had perspective and could place the day's events into a larger picture. They became the keeper of the vision for their settings and understood where their group was in relation to long-term goals. One told me that even after five years, the school was less than half way to its goals. This was neither good nor bad news; it was simply an objective reading.

*Trusting but not naive.* These leaders were more than interested in the ideas of those around them; they knew that they depended upon others every day. They had great trust in teachers, students, staff, and parents. However, they combined this faith with a sophisticated understanding of how organizations work. A friend of one principal told me how this person knew which kinds of curricular decisions needed consensus and which needed to be made alone. Leaders frequently spoke about the stages of idea development they used and where a given project was in relation to that stage. They also showed a grasp of subtlety, knowing when to try a new idea or when caution was best. Some reminded me of great leaders such as Franklin Roosevelt; they seemed to enjoy being a leader just as he did.

*Powerful but not overbearing.* One of the leaders was described as "one of those rare principals who understands that her job is to make safe space for the staff." A teacher in a different building told me, "I get support from the top." Teachers and students in these settings knew that their leader was in charge, but they saw that person as passing power on to others. This came in the form of support, encouragement, and establishing frameworks to set new directions.

*Visible but quiet.* At each site I was given an initial tour, in most cases by the leader. The leaders traveled through the corridors as if they were taking me through their home, stopping frequently for informal conversations with students or teachers. It was clear that these were not people who stayed in their offices all day. Yet, they were also careful not to interrupt the life of their schools.

*Dignified but informal.* Some leaders were referred to as "Mr.," "Ms.," or "Mrs.," even by teachers and staff, but none of the leaders was stuffy. Leadership was not a tuxedo or evening gown that they wore to impress; it came from inside and it was subtle. Their offices had comfortable, informal chairs that communicated a great deal about the kinds of encounters they preferred. For example, Jerry Locke, principal of Burruss Elementary, had two large rockers placed side by side in front of his desk. He likes to sit next to a visitor, whether a teacher, parent, or student. That setting symbolized this group's style of work.

*Demanding but understanding.* These leaders expected very high levels of performance from everyone in the organization. Usually they hired people who came to the setting with a history of achievement. This meant that to realize high expectations, these leaders had to practice excellent listening skills. Remarks like "He listens to me and lets me make decisions" were common.

*Highly ambitious—but for their group, not themselves.* One way the leaders expressed the ambitions they had for their organizations was by being a bridge to the larger world. Kaye Egan, principal of Sinclair Secondary School, told me that there could be no changes in isolation. Therefore, she gets her staff out and about for training and conferences. This pattern was apparent throughout the sites. Above all, these leaders had a sense of personal efficacy. They knew that they had the power to make a difference, and they did this best by transmitting power to those who work with them: teachers, staff, students, parents, community members, and businesspeople.

The leaders of 8 of the 10 sites had come up through the district's system. The two superintendents were both practicing in their home state. These schools and districts had a wonderful supply of talent to tap, and, in turn, these leaders saw their own staffs as sources of leadership. They tended to help those they led become leaders in their own sphere, and they encouraged the development of these 10 traits in others. Carolyn Harden, principal of Oak Grove

Elementary School in the Northeast Arkansas School District, revealed this tendency as she explained how she helped a new idea get started or how she encouraged her staff to travel for new ideas. She displayed a sense of appreciation for those around her as she spoke about her close relations with students and their families in a community in which she had grown up. These values were also apparent in Lee Vent, the district superintendent. Stable conditions and effective leadership seem to be crucial elements in initiating a climate friendly to curriculum leadership. Of equal importance is a strategic vision that connects curriculum, instruction, and assessment together in a living model.

## Curriculum, Instruction, and Assessment: A Dynamic System

We now have a description of the preconditions that enable schools and districts to launch into new directions from a stable base, and a list of important leadership qualities. Comparing curriculum leadership to flying, we may have a solid runway long enough for takeoff and we may know what a qualified pilot is like, but how do we control the aircraft in the first place? In our case, the basic controls are the core operations of curriculum, instruction, and assessment. One early step for curriculum leaders is to develop an understanding of these three and how they work together.

The need to connect curriculum, instruction, and assessment into a system and to understand the way that system operates may seem obvious—after all, these are the basic functions of any school. Yet, I felt obliged to work through this problem because I faced an enigma as I reconstructed the development of curriculum leadership at these schools and districts. As I traced their work, I found no absolute starting place from which they all had begun. The issue seemed far from obvious.

In the state of Vermont, for instance, assessment in the form of portfolios in mathematics and writing came first, but these soon led to discussions of instructional techniques and finally to the Vermont Common Core of Learning. Sinclair Secondary School has placed great emphasis on instructional development, especially the use of cooperative learning. Yet, work is also proceeding on an interdisciplinary 9th grade program with clear implications for curriculum and assessment. Three Oaks Elementary School adopted E.D. Hirsch's Core Knowledge curriculum but found itself enriching instruction and finding new ways for students to share their learning (new assessment strategies). I needed a model that would explain how schools might start with development in either curriculum, instruction, or assessment and end up paying attention to the remaining two.

### The CIA Rubber Band Triangle: Connecting the Elements

Curriculum (the learning agenda), instruction (how we work with learners to understand the agenda), and assessment (how we help learners see their progress in reaching the agenda) have been described as a triangle.[1] If we named each point, it would become the C (curriculum) I (instruction) A (assessment) triangle. The interior of the CIA triangle could be called the "area of learner development."

This triangle helps to illustrate the concept that curriculum, instruction, and assessment are linked and relate to learners. But the relationship of these three elements has a dynamic quality that can best be seen if we modify the model somewhat. First, we need to make the legs of the triangle stretchable—creating what we might call a "CIA rubber band triangle." This will allow us to expand the area of learner development. Second, we need to remember that the elements of curriculum, instruction, and assessment work best together if they are in balance or if they can be diagramed as an equilateral triangle. Thus, we might pull the curriculum point of the triangle by working on that element. If we pull hard enough, the triangle will become isosceles. The curriculum will be developed, but instruction and assessment will remain as they were. To regain balance among the elements, we must pay attention to those two. In this

---

[1]Hilda Taba (1962) uses a kind of double triangle to describe Virgil Herrick and Ralph Tyler's concept of the relationship among objectives, subject matter, methods of organization, and evaluation. Fenwick English (1988) uses the triangle concept to isolate the written, tested, and taught curriculum for the purpose of curriculum auditing. Finally, English and Robert Larson (1996) use the triangle again to describe work design (the curriculum), work (instruction), and work assessment (learning).

way we again have an equilateral CIA triangle—but with a much larger area of learner development. (See Figure 1.1.)

---

FIGURE 1.1.

## THE CIA RUBBER BAND TRIANGLE

1. If we say that curriculum, instruction, and assessment work together and must be in balance, then they can be depicted as the points of an equilateral triangle. The interior of the triangle represents the area of learner development.

2. If we stretch one of the elements (for example, by working on the curriculum), the triangle is no longer balanced.

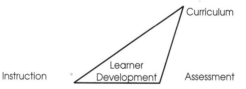

3. To regain balance among the elements, we must work on the remaining two legs of the triangle. In this way we again have an equilateral CIA triangle, but with a much larger area of learner development.

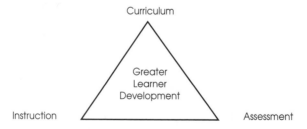

Note: It does not matter which one of the elements is worked on first. Schools generally begin by working on the element of the triangle that offers some freedom to maneuver.

---

Like a rule of nature, the CIA rubber band triangle allows for dynamic change no matter what the starting point. This explains why curriculum quickly became an issue in Vermont. With the spotlight on portfolio assessment, people started to ask about the content of student writing. It also explains how Sinclair's intensive work on cooperative learning (an instructional issue) enabled new interdisciplinary ideas (a curriculum issue) to take root. After all, if one of the reasons for cooperative learning is to break down student isolation, why not break down some of the isolation of the academic disciplines? Finally, the CIA rubber band triangle, which always favors balance among the three elements, explains how Three Oaks Elementary School changed instruction after it worked on curriculum. Teachers felt free to explore new instructional practices because the Core Knowledge curriculum was in place and agreed to. They could focus their energy elsewhere.

The CIA triangle is comparable to the basic controls of the aircraft. Understanding how the three elements operate is like saying, "These are the controls: push the stick forward to go down, pull back to go up; use the foot controls and the stick to bank to the left or the right." But every flight school also provides a dose of theory. You may know how to move the stick and the foot pedals, but why do they work? We may be able to understand that the elements of curriculum, instruction, and assessment are dynamically linked, but what causes this?

### THE YIN-YANG METAPHOR:
#### WHY CURRICULUM, INSTRUCTION, AND ASSESSMENT ARE LINKED

To understand the link among curriculum, instruction, and assessment, we need to shift the metaphor from a triangle to what I call a modified yin-yang. Those who have studied Asian culture may be familiar with the yin-yang symbol. Looking like two intertwined paisleys, one usually white, one usually black, it depicts the unity of opposites. This can mean the connection between light and dark, such as night and day. Westerners may find the concept of the unity of opposites ironic because in the West opposites have typically been described as diametrically opposed enemies. Thus, light occurs in one place and darkness in the opposite place. But the principle of yin-yang suggests that these two seeming opposites are actually connected, and the cycle of day and night provides a simple but powerful example.

Yin-yang goes further by stating that each element contains a piece of its opposite. That is why a white dot appears in the black part of the yin-yang symbol, and a black dot in the white part. The night may be dark, but the moon and the stars are a reminder of day-time's brightness. The day may be light, but the sun is only one of many stars, and the clouds can be so thick that midday can seem like dusk. Yin-yang can provide a new way to see the forces in the world, a way that binds them to one another in a dynamic tension. Taking this conception into the problem of curriculum, instruction, and assessment requires only one step. Instead of the two elements of yin-yang, we need three. This would give us a modified yin-yang, with one part for each of the three areas and two dots in each area (see Figure 1.2). The element of curriculum has a small bit of instruction and a small bit of assessment in it. Assessment has a small piece of instruction and a small piece of curriculum in it. Instruction has a small bit of curriculum and a small bit of assessment in it. Anyone who has worked in assessment, curriculum, or instruction might easily see how the principle of the modified yin-yang operates in practice. I have recently come across three examples myself.

A teacher in a small school called me one day in a bit of a panic. "Steve," she said in a tense voice, "I've really started to work on the changes in instruction you spoke about. My students are much more active and my projects are much more creative. But now I have to give report cards. What can I do? We do not have a way to show this new stuff." She had worked in the realm of instruction, but a built-in question of assessment had now appeared. I gave her some ideas for her immediate problem, but if we had expanded the conversation we would have come to the question of the learning agenda—the curriculum—itself, because it too is built into instruction.

The teachers at the Heron Institute faced the same problem. They labored to create hands-on science and math experiences—an instructional development—which meant that they had to devise ways to help their students show their learning—an assessment issue. They also pondered the content of student learning, which turned the question into a curricular issue.

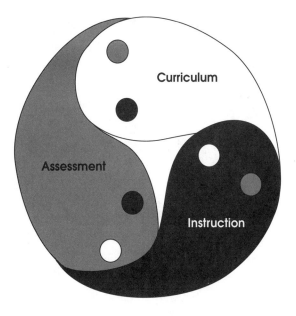

**FIGURE 1.2.**

**A MODIFIED YIN-YANG FOR CURRICULUM, ASSESSMENT, AND INSTRUCTION**

Each one of the three interrelated elements—curriculum, instruction, and assessment—has bits of the other two in it.

Illustration concept by Will Gross.

The Cabot School spent a great deal of time creating a profile of graduates, which had a big impact on curriculum. Quickly, people saw important questions of instruction (how shall we help learners engage the curriculum?) and assessment (how well are learners reaching the goals we have agreed to?). In Cabot's case, curriculum had an element of instruction and assessment.

The modified yin-yang model explains why the three elements—curriculum, instruction, and assessment—always move toward balance or harmony. Like understanding the principles of lift and drag as they apply to flight, it is the theory that explains why our flight controls work as they do.

We now have a better background to understand how these sites got "off the ground" in general terms. It's time to map the different routes they took on the way to curriculum leadership.

## Four Paths to Curriculum Leadership

Understanding the dynamic relationship among curriculum, instruction, and assessment will help launch the curriculum leadership process, just as learning the flight controls of the airplane will allow a plane to taxi and take off. But once airborne, what direction should be taken? If the general flight plan is to head toward greater learning for all students, what territory does the school have to fly over? What is the weather likely to be on the way? Formally and informally, leaders and their teams study their environment to make what amounts to a flight plan. Because of their different situations and the differing styles of their leaders, the sites each set their own course. However, these can be grouped into four large categories:

- Starting fresh
- Bringing home a new idea
- Agreeing to take a journey
- Establishing a mechanism to unleash innovation

### STARTING FRESH

Starting a new school may be the greatest dream of teachers and administrators. Only a few ever get that opportunity. Three of the 10 sites in this study had just such a chance.

#### SINCLAIR SECONDARY SCHOOL

When the Durham Board of Education asked Kaye Egan to leave her post as a successful high school principal and help plan a new school, she took the opportunity to explore. First she met with Toronto-area principals who also were planning new schools and read books and articles with them. She then visited several school districts in Vancouver to explore new possibilities for curriculum. "We got a chance to find out what kids were learning, how curriculum was being delivered, and how the design was different than what I had ever imagined." She found that people in other settings were acting differently from her expectations, yet they were succeeding. "It gave me courage to say I think we too can strike out and be different." She found out what the schools were most proud of, as well as how these innovative schools shared their ideas with their communities.

Coming back to Toronto, Egan discussed her findings with the vice principals, the head of guidance, and the head of media—all people who were already on board. This core team expanded as the school hired department heads. The group developed concrete plans for the new school, such as a sophisticated technology infrastructure that would connect all of the classes to the media center. The group also started to create a philosophy and a value system. "That's how I built support for my basic philosophy and my beliefs and values." For Kaye Egan and her team, recent training in cooperative management, provincial openness to some curriculum integration in the 9th grade, and an opportunity to see working models that emphasized new curricular directions and technology designs helped to make the most of "a rare chance to make a fresh start."

As their ideas developed, Egan and her team met with parents from around the district. Because their school was not yet built, they held the meetings at the sender schools, and they included an invitation to join a curriculum committee. Parents could offer their ideas and work on areas of the curriculum they were interested in. This simple strategy made the difference between an undesirable outcome—ill-focused meetings centered on when the sidewalk concrete would be poured—and a desirable outcome—working meetings that resulted in clear curriculum directions. Principal Egan reported that about 250 parents joined a curriculum committee and worked throughout the summer to help refine the school's plan. These parents became Sinclair's first community contacts.

## OCEANA HIGH SCHOOL

Like Kaye Egan, Lois Jones was a well-respected administrator. She had been part of Oceana High School for many years as a guidance counselor and then as an assistant principal. Just as Egan's original school was known for solid performance, Oceana was respected for delivering a good, if traditional, education. In 1991 Jones was asked to assume the principalship and only a few months later was asked to close down the original Oceana and lay plans for a very different kind of school to be housed in the same building. She too was given a chance to make a fresh start.

Also like Egan, Jones worked with a small team to invent the new enterprise. In the evenings her group planned and dreamed about the future. During the day, they had to return to a school that was going out of existence. Because the new Oceana, like Sinclair, was going to start out much smaller than surrounding schools, it was clear that not everyone in the old school would be able to stay. Thus, Jones and her group not only had to hide their enthusiasm for their new plans, they also had to help nervous colleagues grieve for the loss of a school that had been part of the community for two decades.

One early source of help for the Oceana team came from a presentation by the Coalition of Essential Schools. As Jones and her group heard the nine Coalition principles, they felt that they were hearing reflections of their own ideas. They decided to seek Coalition membership. Like her Canadian colleague, Principal Jones also brought the community into the process of building the learning agenda for her new school.

### SQUIRES ELEMENTARY SCHOOL

Jay Jordan, principal of Squires Elementary School in Lexington, Kentucky, got his fresh start in a somewhat different way. Like the others in this category of fresh-start schools, Squires was held in high regard by families. However, the Kentucky Education Reform Act (KERA) thoroughly revamped public education in the state in the early 1990s, with a major impact on school finance, governance, assessment, and curriculum. KERA also gave local schools a decisive role in curriculum decisions, as well as a push toward the creation of an ungraded primary unit. Instead of teaching in isolation, teachers were asked to form communities of children.

At first, Jordan was incensed by this directive, because he thought that the real problem was at the high school level. Thinking the matter through further, however, he decided that if the ungraded primary unit was coming anyway, it might as well be done correctly. He joined the Primary Institute sponsored by the University of Kentucky, which was an early vehicle for expanding his knowledge of such issues as multi-age classes, and he and his group visited models in Kentucky and beyond. The UCLA Lab School, demonstrating John Goodlad's early work with ungraded elementary classes, impressed him and helped him make a shift in direction that is common to all 10 sites: *Learning rather than teaching needs to be at the center of the school's existence.*

The fresh-start schools got their impetus from above. In two of the cases, the district board and administration provided the opportunity. In the third instance, the turnover of an entire state's education system provided a willing principal with the chance to make decisive changes. This by no means diminishes the importance of the hard creative work it took to get Sinclair, Oceana, and Squires off the ground. Getting a chance to start a new school is wonderful, but it is only an opportunity. Setting the forces of change in motion, finding helpful models, linking with a supportive network, and creating a collaborative new design are the acts of a truly gifted leadership team. But what if a school is not in a position to start from scratch? In what other ways can serious curriculum change begin? To what extent can the principal set a new course? Let's look next at the central role a respected leader can play.

### Bringing Home a New Idea

Three of the schools started their road to curriculum leadership because of a new idea brought home by the principal. Although in these cases the principal initiated the change effort, implementation was clearly a team effort.

### Three Oaks Elementary School

Connie Jones had been a successful 5th grade teacher before opening the Three Oaks Elementary School near Fort Myers, Florida, in 1988. Like the principals of the schools getting a fresh start, Jones had a strong voice in the hiring of new staff and could select people who were known for high energy, great past performance, and a capacity for continuous growth. Three Oaks was in a slightly different situation than the schools in the fresh-start category in one way: Elementary schools in Lee County had developed the tradition of taking on specific themes that were approved by the director of elementary education. For example, some schools focused on the environment, others concentrated on science and technology.

For Dr. Jones, this was a unique chance to put the ideas of E.D. Hirsch into practice. She had used Hirsch's *Cultural Literacy* (1988) in a graduate course on curriculum she was coteaching, and she found that the idea of systematically studying major historic, literary, scientific, and artistic content had strong appeal. She had long been concerned that children were not benefiting from the advantages of a well-structured learning plan. She could control much of what they learned in her 5th grade classroom, but what they learned before or after was largely a matter of guesswork. She felt that the district curriculum guides were simply too vague. Phrases like "a lover of literature" or "an understanding of historical events" were fine, but *what* literature was to be studied? *Which* historical events mattered most? With no such agreement, especially in science and social studies, children repeated some topics such as Native Americans and missed others altogether. Hirsch's cultural literacy concept seemed like a good way to solve the problem.

Jones brought the idea to the county board of education and got permission to head her new school toward the cultural literacy path. Because no other school in the nation was using these ideas and there were no formal curriculum documents to follow, Three Oaks had to start with small steps. Teachers read Hirsch's book and selected items from its contents. According to Jones, their work was still somewhat random. The 1,000 students at Three Oaks received a good skills background, however content consistency remained problematic. For example, one teacher might conduct a great unit on the Vikings or the rain forest; but as Jones observed, "the teachers did not trade units. . . . consequently, depending on which teacher a child got, they could have an entirely different knowledge base." And the teacher who did such a great job with the rain forest unit might not offer it the following year. Great books such as *Charlotte's Web* might be read three times in different classes during a child's elementary education, yet other classics would be ignored. As the staff moved to instructional innovations such as whole language and thematic units, the problem became more obvious because the consistency that the basal readers had provided was gone. Jones and her staff faced a dilemma: They liked the newer ways of teaching, but they were concerned by the lack of a logically sequenced curriculum for all of their students.

Then in the spring of 1990, Hirsch and his colleagues held a conference at the University of Virginia to refine a scope-and-sequence list of topics that matched the ideals of cultural literacy. Jones became one of the 100 guests, who included teachers, textbook writers, and politicians. Their charge was to help analyze and reshape the list over the course of several days. The original list provided by Hirsch's team provided a jumping-off place. The group broke into smaller teams that had to reach consensus before they could pass an idea on to the larger group. In turn, the large group needed to reach consensus on all points. After three days of careful work and enthusiastic debates, the list of topics by grade—the Core Knowledge curriculum—was complete. The conference did not deal with methods of instruction or with assessment, which were left to the discretion of the sites.

With this list in hand and with the understanding that the new Core Knowledge curriculum was intended to account for only 50 percent of classroom time, Jones came back to her school and asked her faculty to move the school in this direction. She organized a Core Knowledge Committee that included classroom teachers from all grade levels as well as arts, media, and special education teachers and the principal. In this forum teachers could debate the merits of the plan and freely admit their need to learn new material in certain fields. The Core Knowledge Committee had roles related to these areas:

- Strategies to organize content into a teaching plan
- Teacher communication between classrooms, disciplines, and grade levels
- Communication with parents
- Lesson plans

- Assessment
- Schoolwide themes, displays, activities, and programs

The committee members worked together to bring a systematic implementation of the Core Knowledge curriculum to Three Oaks.

### HANSBERRY ELEMENTARY SCHOOL

Montrose Spencer was an assistant principal before she became principal of Hansberry Elementary School in the South Bronx. Hansberry was created to relieve overcrowding. Like Three Oaks, it occupied a new building and had a new staff. Early innovations included a whole language approach to children's literature. Then, in 1993, the school was approached by the Hudson Institute's Modern Red Schoolhouse project. Spencer already believed in such key principles of the project as parent and community involvement, concentrated use of technology, and attention to the curriculum. Hansberry became a Modern Red Schoolhouse school, and Spencer formed a leadership team to guide the project.

Spencer's team divided into subgroups that worked on all major project areas. The curriculum, like that of Three Oaks, was based on E.D. Hirsch's Core Knowledge plan. At Hansberry, teams of teachers took the Core Knowledge topics and created what are called Hudson Units around the themes. Spencer and her staff were then able to connect their curricular ideas to district, city, and state expectations. While the Modern Red Schoolhouse project took an important early step in inviting Hansberry to join their project, Montrose Spencer and her staff played a crucial role in moving their school in this new direction. They created what one teacher calls "a problem-solving place."

### BURRUSS ELEMENTARY SCHOOL

Burruss Elementary School was known for providing a solid education for children in its section of Marietta, Georgia. Principal Jerry Locke and his staff had worked well together for several years at another school before Burruss was built. When Locke moved into the new school, he brought most of his staff with him. They were known as a hard-working and high-achieving group. Because the school had to follow Georgia's Quality Core Curriculum, many basic decisions of content were already made. Yet the structure provided for considerable latitude.

Locke began to move his school in a new direction after he attended a meeting of the League of Professional Schools at the University of Georgia. This organization, under the leadership of Carl Glickman, emphasized the idea that meaningful change comes from within the schools themselves, not from the outside. Locke appreciated the emphasis on action research and shared governance as well. Under Locke's guidance, Burruss joined the League. This opened new channels of support and sharing for his staff, as well as "the realization that maybe there were some other things out there that we want to bring back."

The first innovation came in the area of whole language. Locke read a report about a language arts program called SUCCESS and was so impressed that he immediately offered the idea to teachers. Because it was the end of the school year, he asked his staff to consider the program over the summer and return the next semester with an opinion. In September every teacher expressed willingness to give the new program a try.

Whether a new school is created or the principal brings home a new plan, the direction for curriculum change seems clear. But sometimes schools and communities find it best to simply start by joining together to pose important questions.

### Agreeing to Take a Journey

The fresh-start group received a blank slate and a mandate from above to create change. For the second group new directions came from a leader who found a specific vehicle for change. A third possibility involves school leaders joining with community and staff to begin a journey. No new school is contemplated, and the leader does not come back to the school with a bold specific direction. Rather, the third option involves a long, detailed group process motivated by a need to improve.

## THE CABOT SCHOOL

Marge Sable was a well-respected principal in her small K–12 school. Even beyond the small town of Cabot, Vermont, she was admired for her energy and dedication. She was also known to be highly committed to her students and their families. Cabot was considered a good school by conventional standards when in 1989 Sable and a cross section of parents, teachers, and board members decided that much more could be done. They looked at their curriculum and decided that they could probably accomplish all of the high school's program by the end of the 11th grade. They wondered what the curriculum would be like if they increased the rigor of the academic disciplines. An important early catalyst for change came when the state of Vermont offered a challenge grant for schools that planned to restructure. The school formed a task force, and the school board gave its permission for the group to write a proposal to compete for one of the state grants.

The planners' premise was that the school belonged to the community. Therefore, parents and businesspeople needed to be involved in setting a new direction. In fact, Sable decided to support the effort but not to attend the evening meetings, thus giving the teachers and community members lots of room to set standards. Another early conviction was that parents and businesspeople would set higher standards for students than teachers would.

Cabot received one of the state grants, the first of several awards it would earn. The planning group spent two years examining the status of the school's program, devising objectives, and setting graduation standards. Leadership's role in this situation was one of knowing when and how to tap into community support, how to bring teachers in on the process in positive ways, when to link up with state and national groups for support, and how to keep the school board invested in the process. Since the process started in 1989, Cabot has been transformed from the inside out.

## THE HERON INSTITUTE

The Heron Institute and the Heron Network in Madison, Wisconsin, represent another example of a group deciding to take a journey together. In this case, the group consists of teachers, mostly in the elementary and middle grades. The group's informal leader, Mark Wagler, explained that Heron had its origins in many small and individual efforts that later led to joint training programs for interested members. Members of the group decided early on that, to teach science differently, they needed to be scientists themselves; if they were going to teach writing, they needed to write. They wanted to teach from mastery, not from an abstract notion that someone brought in from the outside and sold to the school. As one of the members said, "We have to change inside of us."

Since 1993, Heron teachers, representing several schools in the Madison area, have studied such subjects as mathematics, whitewater ecology, telecommunications, and multimedia. They remain a cohesive group through informal meetings in which members share experiences, solve specific problems, and plan for professional development. In their presence it is easy to see what Aronowitz and Giroux (1991) mean by the phrase "teachers as the public's intellectuals."

## ESTABLISHING A MECHANISM TO UNLEASH INNOVATION

The first three sets of examples—fresh starts, new directions from the school leader, and taking a journey together—all center on school change originating at the building or classroom level. But what can a district do to increase the likelihood of curriculum innovation? Here the emphasis is less on the central design of "some right answer" and more on the establishment of dynamic processes that unleash invention at the school sites. The Northeast Arkansas School District in Paragould and the Verona School District in Wisconsin offer two good, yet different, examples of how this works.

## THE NORTHEAST ARKANSAS SCHOOL DISTRICT

A new system of curriculum development started in the Northeast Arkansas School District in 1990. At that time, a large local manufacturer began to train its employees in total quality management (TQM). The superintendent of schools, Lee Vent, received an invitation to send a representative to the training. When Leon Lowe, the director of curriculum for the district, came back with an enthusiastic report on the training experience, Vent and other district leaders worked to bring TQM training to area teachers and administrators. In the spring of 1991, nearby Harding University designed a version of TQM for school personnel. Administrators were the first to be trained, followed by teachers and board members. Now, all new employees must receive training. In Vent's view, the organizational philosophy of TQM gave the sites a sense of ownership. With less hierarchy in the system, people at the building level felt able to apply for grants and start new initiatives. They no longer felt that they needed permission to invent.

Encouraged to think of whole new ways to reach students and their families, the teachers and administrators at the schools went to work. But merely tacking new programs onto the curriculum without a framework for reflection and evaluation can lead to chaos. Vent described the cycle of project development in place in the district to respond to that potential problem.

First, an idea comes on the scene. If it receives a small degree of interest, it can be tested at one site where data can be gathered over the course of a year. Then the project is subject to evaluation. Should it continue? Should it be carried to other sites and thereby become institutionalized? Not all good ideas are going to work in every setting for any number of reasons, but this system provides a reasonable opportunity for trial, testing, and analysis based upon objective information.

Project Mast, an interdisciplinary program for mathematics and science, offers a good illustration of the cycle. After hearing about the program, the district sent two interested teachers to the University of Arkansas for five weeks of training. Then, in the fall of 1991, two model classes were set up. After being evaluated as a success, the district institutionalized the program. Every classroom from 2nd to 5th grade now uses this approach. Vent explained that the key element in the process is teacher ownership of ideas. When it comes to a program idea for 1st graders, for example, "Who can tell me about the needs of the 1st grade classroom better than the 1st grade teachers?"

Lee Vent's approach was so successful that the challenges this district faced involved dividing the wheat from the chaff of the good ideas that sprang to life. In four years, teachers, administrators, and community members in the Northeast Arkansas School District came up with more than 60 major programs, including aquaculture, summer enhancement, school-to-work, and a literature program called Sing Spell Read Write. With the key elements for district invention, testing, and decision making in place, the district has moved decisively to correct the overabundance of new ideas.

## THE VERONA SCHOOL DISTRICT

In Verona, Wisconsin, community division over the general direction of the district's learning program caused deep reflection and change at all levels. A former superintendent of schools was able to start a powerful strategic planning process and initiate a number of important innovations. According to some administrators and community members, problems developed because not enough of the community was brought along, and as a result, serious divisions began to emerge. The goals of the district have since been modified to reflect the input of many more people in the community, and the pace of change has slowed down to take into consideration the concerns of the families and businesses in the area.

But how can this be done without forsaking progress? Bob Gilpatrick, superintendent of schools, and Linda Christensen, director of instruction, explained their transition from a linear planning model with specific future goals and corresponding action plans to a process of broad-based community involvement around areas of interest. These areas of interest include technology, district curriculum planning, financial planning structure, governance, and new facilities. This constitutes the framework of the district's development, but the boundaries of the framework are not rigid; they allow for change in midcourse. By inviting everyone in the organization and beyond into the creative process, the district can allow for people's strengths to guide their work. As in Northeast Arkansas, the positive side of gaining people's creative energies must be weighed against the dangers of a poorly coordinated curriculum plan. What happens, district leaders wonder, when the diverse curriculum that children experience in elementary school creates different levels of readiness for the middle school or high school? How can flexibility be balanced with consistency of quality? These are problems that Verona as a community is considering as it moves, in Superintendent Gilpatrick's words, from being a school system to a system of schools.

## Size and Finances

Regardless of how they began their involvement in curriculum leadership, all of the sites faced some of the same pragmatic questions. What size should the school be? What will this mean for staff? What strategy can be used to accomplish goals and still stay within the budget? It helps to look at the ways these sites grew into their new roles.

### Starting Small

In the cases of school starting fresh, district administrators agreed to phase in growth over several years. This enabled Oceana to start its first year as a redesigned school with only 325 students. Over the next five years that number grew to nearly 800, and it may go higher. Sinclair started as a new school with 800 students. In the second year it grew to 1,200, with an expectation of 1,600 students in the third year. The Hansberry School started small and now has close to 500 students.

A small student population at the start meant that fewer faculty members were required. Hansberry set out to become a Modern Red Schoolhouse with only a dozen teachers. Oceana was in a similar position. Sinclair had a larger, but still relatively small, group. These schools considered their hiring decisions to be immensely important. Principals talked about conducting hundreds of interviews before school opened. At Sinclair the number reached 500, all from within the system. At Oceana, Lois Jones captured the qualities of the kind of person that most of these schools wanted: a sense of excitement, flexibility, a caring attitude toward students, and the ability to do more than one thing. Other qualities mentioned by principals included the ability to work well within a team, knowledge of subject matter, and knowledge of several instructional strategies.

It must be noted that Sinclair hired teachers from within the Durham Board and that teachers from the old Oceana not selected for the new Oceana were given jobs elsewhere in the district. Thus, new schools did not have to live in the shadow of labor disputes.

These schools were looking for highly dynamic people who had already demonstrated their creativity, but they did not insist on hiring only veteran teachers. Several highly successful teachers at Three Oaks Elementary, for instance, had only a few years of experience. Some had never taught in a different setting. At Hansberry, a core group of teachers had made a midcareer switch from business to education. Candidates for positions at all of the schools needed to show that they were active and inventive; the schools avoided teachers who preferred to work alone.

Of course, the number of faculty positions in these schools will grow as student population grows, thus giving the original planners the important job of ensuring that newcomers understand the goals of the school. Faculty expansion also allows the schools to incorporate the good ideas that new people bring.

Curriculum innovation in schools and districts that did not get a fresh start also started out as a small enterprise. The Northeast Arkansas District experiments on a small scale, as does the Verona School District, with its new charter schools. The Heron Group moves in small steps with new ideas, as does the Cabot School with innovations such as a senior exhibition project. Burruss Elementary School experiments in small ways with its new ideas in curriculum, often launching new programs as extracurricular activities through its PTA. All of these represent versions of the same wisdom of allowing ideas time to mature and giving community members, teachers, and students the chance to get used to innovation. This practice also gives each innovation a home base and built-in supporters. It is important to note, as mentioned earlier, that programs need to justify themselves at regular intervals according to commonly accepted standards.

## FINANCES

The sites created curriculum innovations without additional operating funds from the district. The range of district spending was, however, quite varied, reflecting regional and national patterns. Some of the financial considerations are difficult to associate with curriculum leadership directly because building projects would have been required in any case for some of the schools. The important thing to realize is that these schools were held to the same standards as neighboring schools, with the possible exception of the brand new schools, which started their existence with fewer students.

However, even these soon reached the same general size as others in their system.

These schools did obtain extra resources through fund-raising and grants. One of the principals called these "booster shots," to be invested heavily in staff development. Schools gained support from local businesses to help with specific projects in which both the school and the business could benefit. Grants, however, had to pass a test before they were pursued. Would this new resource bring the school closer to a particular goal or not? These schools avoided even large grants that were seen as tangential to their mission.

One more observation needs to be made in the area of finances. Because of their clear direction for learners, these schools and districts had agreed-upon criteria on which to base budget decisions. As Marge Sable explained, once Cabot had agreed to use student learning in relation to school standards as its highest goal, priorities became easier to set. Even when purchasing supplies, she could pose the question, "Does this item help us reach our standards or not?" This kind of centered thinking played an even more crucial role in much larger issues, such as the need for a technology expert instead of an industrial arts teacher.

These schools and districts have developed a sensitive and strategic process for initiating curriculum change. Part of that subtle process involves finding an important place for community participation early on.

## The Community's Early Role

Contact with the community is not an add-on for these sites; it is an integral part of how they do their work. For some, the idea of community ownership of the schools was a stated part of their core beliefs from the first planning meetings. For others, it has been an evolving relationship. In either case, the roots of community involvement go far back. All of the sites have moved beyond merely telling families that they are important.

For Cabot, Oceana, and Sinclair, community involvement started almost at once. Cabot's use of a community task force has already been described; a look at the other two reveals similar patterns. At

Oceana, Lois Jones and her core group of teachers started to work with parents, students, businesspeople, and community members immediately. This cross section formed the Academic Council, which began its work by establishing the new school's Learning Outcomes. As defined by this group, Oceana graduates would be proficient in basic skills of communication (reading, writing, listening, and speaking), mathematics, and physical fitness; they would be problem solvers who know how to visualize solutions; they would be creative, reflective, and critical thinkers; they would be able to work independently and with others cooperatively to accomplish tasks; and they would be respectful of themselves, other people, and other cultures.

At Sinclair, community action came from the PTA in the form of what became known as the Parent School Advisory. In the school's first year of operation, the group decided to concentrate its efforts on student learning and came up with this list of outcomes: independent and confident individual; collaborative worker; technology information manager; effective communicator; healthy, active individual; conscientious global citizen; complex thinker; artistic learner. The list came from discussions with administrators, parents, community members, and students. The staff and principal helped to organize the advisory's meetings. The group started with major topics and members filled in the details, retaining commonly shared ideas. By organizing the Parent School Advisory early on, Sinclair put into place the forerunner of the Community Councils that are now mandated in Ontario.

Community members at these schools were able to provide helpful direction. Yet it is important to remember that community involvement is a process that evolves. Early goal setting with the community seems to result in general statements such as the ones above. These statements are useful, but even more significant, they are often the first examples of cooperative planning between the school and outside groups. At some of the sites, community involvement became very focused and detailed for about two years and then diminished. This was the case at Cabot, where the task force apparently felt its mandate was fulfilled once the school's direction was established. For Oceana and Sinclair, community involvement to set learning goals was a first step, followed by formal, ongoing committee work that includes parents and business representatives.

Parental advice was crucial in shaping the ungraded primary program at Squires Elementary School. Jay Jordan and his staff were able to design the fundamentals of a new program, but they were sure that it could be refined before they tried to implement it. In January of the year before the plan was to go into effect, they invited parents in for a presentation and general discussion. Parents were willing to consider the new primary program, but they had many questions that first needed to be answered. Jordan took the ideas and concerns raised at the meeting back to his faculty and reworked the plan. In May they presented the same group with a second version of their ungraded primary plan. Jordan was a bit nervous because they had already planned to have about 124 students in the new program. What if none of the parents wanted to let their children try out this experimental idea? His fears soon subsided. By the end of the meeting the families' approval of the project was clear, and the ungraded primary program had a waiting list.

Setting out in a new direction with community support does not always mean asking community members to invent a vision. In the case of Three Oaks, families responded to the Core Knowledge curriculum with enthusiasm—and a little surprise. In effect, they told Connie Jones, "This is good, but isn't this what schools always have done?" Ironically, it was the faculty that debated the plan. Some wondered whether young children could understand such subjects as ancient Egypt. At Burruss, new curricular directions have been set in an evolutionary way. Because the school has won state and national awards for excellence and because it is involved in such programs as the Program for School Improvement, community support is considered solid.

There are limits to the kind of direction that community members can give to schools. Developing problem-solving skills, communication abilities, and facility in working with others is well within the range of most groups. Community members can also respond to direct proposals, such as the ungraded primary program at Squires or the Core Knowledge curriculum at Three Oaks. Given time, community groups can transform into a task force that can be a powerful partner with administrators and school board in setting a brand new direction, as happened at Cabot. Time will also allow community members to serve effectively on advisory boards that have serious duties in academic decision making. This has happened at Oceana and Sinclair. But in the early phases, this kind of detailed planning seems beyond most groups. As Chapter 4 will show, although community involvement could not prevent turbulence at Sinclair or in Verona, both systems were far stronger as a result of the community support they did have, albeit imperfect.

Clearly, the early phases of curriculum leadership are busy ones. The leader must possess important traits, the school must be stable, and planners must understand how curriculum, instruction, and assessment relate to one another. Next, planners must use this understanding and knowledge of their own conditions to select an appropriate flight path. Finally, curriculum leadership involves new staffing, financial decisions, and community involvement. But with all of this groundwork established, what plans do these schools use? What are some of today's most successful curriculum plans like? To answer these questions we will now take a close look at the curriculum choices these schools and districts have made.

## Consider for a Moment

As you think about curriculum leadership in your setting, you may find these questions helpful:

- How well does your school match the Four Preconditions of Curriculum Leadership?
- How do your leader's skills compare with the 10 Qualities of Curriculum Leaders? Which qualities may need development?
- Where may you need to strengthen your existing program? What "flight path" best fits your school or district situation? How might others in your organization see things? You may want to consider yourself in year zero, thereby taking time to prepare your organization for the tasks ahead.

# Successful Curriculum Plans

Before there can be a rational curriculum, we must
settle which things it most concerns us to know. . . .
we must determine the relative value of
knowledges.
—HERBERT SPENCER, *WHAT KNOWLEDGE IS OF MOST WORTH*, 1860

Understanding how schools and districts approach curriculum leadership and initiate the process of becoming something new is crucial.
We have considered leadership, the preconditions of stability that
permit serious departures to take place, the relationship between the
core elements of curriculum, instruction, and assessment, and the
variety of styles schools and districts use to start their exploration.
But what of the curriculum plans themselves? It is now time to examine some of the choices that exist for curriculum leaders. What
should the learning agenda be? How should the school's plan fit district and state expectations? What underlying belief systems seem to
be at work as people develop their plans? Finally, how does everything fit together into a coherent program?

All 10 sites have developed complex systems of curriculum over
a span of several years. Because of their evolutionary nature, placing
the sites into a single category is difficult, but key similarities and
contrasts do exist. I have chosen to divide the 10 sites into three large
categories, each reflecting the thrust of their work. These categories
are the following:

- The adopters, whose plans originated from beyond the site.
- The evolvers, whose plans developed from state mandates.
- The developers, whose plans were largely designed at the site.

Please understand, however, that all of the sites did some adopting, some evolving, and some developing.

Through this analysis, the story of curriculum design may be viewed systematically, thereby giving planners an important tool to determine where and how they might start. For instance, leaders need to understand their position along the continuum between loose and tight state mandates in curriculum and adjust accordingly. Oceana High School built the expectations of the California university system and the guidelines of the California curriculum frameworks into its curriculum plan. Looking at provincial requirements, Sinclair Secondary School found room to maneuver in the 9th grade and focused its attention there. Burruss Elementary had to deal with very specific state curriculum expectations, which meant that development started in the area of instructional innovation and spread later into curriculum changes. The Cabot School, on the other hand, was under little pressure from the state or district and had an open horizon. Whether operating under a small patch of blue sky or almost limitless visibility, the common quality of these schools and districts was their willingness to proceed. None of the sites used the expectations from above as an excuse to do nothing.

## The Adopters

At first, adopting a curriculum sounds easy. But as anyone who has tried to bring home a great new idea can attest, adopting a new program requires preparation, faculty acceptance, community acceptance, and resources—just to start. Schools that adopted curriculum plans included Three Oaks Elementary School, Hansberry Elementary School, and Squires Elementary School. Three Oaks was the first school in the United States to use the Core Knowledge curriculum, which originated with E.D. Hirsch's writings on cultural literacy. Hansberry also uses Core Knowledge but adds other elements that are central to the Modern Red Schoolhouse program sponsored by the Hudson Institute. Squires has adopted the Different Ways of Knowing Curriculum developed by the Galef Institute.

### THREE OAKS: PIONEERING THE CORE KNOWLEDGE CURRICULUM

As we have seen, several features attracted Connie Jones and the teachers at Three Oaks to the Core Knowledge curriculum. First, it requires that students follow a coherent pathway through subjects from 1st grade through 6th.[1] Next, the curriculum is designed to create a balance in the elementary years between skills, which the curriculum designers saw as typically receiving significant attention, and content, which they saw as being treated with insufficient continuity. Third, because Core Knowledge applies to everyone, equity between special education students and general education students is more easily approached (see Chapter 3 for more information on special education and Core Knowledge). Finally, the hope exists that if all students receive a Core Knowledge education, the problem of rapid student turnover and corresponding gaps in their education at different schools can be diminished. Much has been written for and against Core Knowledge, and it is not my intention to enter the fray. It is important, however, to understand the broad outlines of this curriculum plan. Figure 2.1 presents a sample of topics studied under Core Knowledge from grades 1 through 6.

### HANSBERRY: BECOMING A MODERN RED SCHOOLHOUSE

As a Modern Red Schoolhouse site, Hansberry uses Core Knowledge to guide its curriculum plan,[2] but that is only part of the picture. Modern Red Schoolhouse schools are founded on what are called the Six Pillars of Reform (Hudson Institute 1995):

1. All children can learn and attain high standards in core academic subjects. Children simply vary in the time they need to learn and the ways they learn best.

---

[1]The sequence originally started in grade 1. Kindergarten has been added in recent years.

[2]At the elementary school, the Core Knowledge cycle applies. For upper grades (7-12), the course content in the Modern Red Schoolhouse plan reflects the idea in the James Madison series developed at the U.S. Department of Education under the leadership of William Bennett as well as national standards developed by professional associations such as the National Council of Teachers of Mathematics (NCTM) standards.

2. Schools should help transmit a common culture that draws on the traditions and histories of our pluralistic society and the principles of liberal democratic government that unite us all. At the same time, all children should understand the cultures and traditions of other nations and peoples.

3. Principals and teachers should have considerable freedom in organizing instruction and deploying resources to meet the needs of their students.

4. Schools should have greater flexibility in deciding how best to accomplish their mission and, at the same time, should be held accountable through regular assessments of student progress.

5. Advanced technology is a critical requisite in attaining high-quality education in cost-effective ways.

6. Schools should be places to which students and staff choose to belong.

Matched to the Core Knowledge curriculum ideas and the six pillars are Standards for Learning that delineate what students should know and be able to do at the end of 4th grade (primary), 8th grade (intermediate), and 12th grade (upper). The Standards are grouped under various Performance Statements. Figure 2.2 presents Performance Statements and examples of Standards for English language arts, geography, history, science, mathematics, foreign language, health and physical education, and fine arts for the primary years.

### THE HUDSON UNIT

Teachers use what are called "Hudson Units" to deliver the Core Knowledge curriculum goals in conjunction with the Performance Statements and Standards. A sample 4th grade Hudson Unit on weather illustrates how this works in practice.

The unit plan starts with 10 large objectives. Under each of these are standards that the objectives are designed to address. Most standards include examples of activities that teachers and students undertake. For example, one objective states: "The students will learn to identify and classify the different types of clouds: a. cirrus; b. stratus; c. cumulus." One of the standards that this objective meets is "Each student can show the conversion of water from a liquid to a solid and

---

FIGURE 2.1.

## SELECTED TOPICS FROM THE CORE KNOWLEDGE CURRICULUM

---

**Grade 1**
- *Literature:* "Sleeping Beauty," Anansi tales, Aesop's Fables, Medio Pollito, "The Frog Prince"
- *Geography:* the seven continents; the equator; the Atlantic and Pacific oceans; north, south, east, west
- *World History:* Ancient Egypt, early religions
- *American History:* early people of the Americas (Maya, Inca, Aztec), Columbus, 4th of July, George Washington
- *Math:* adding and subtracting to 12, counting money, greater than and less than, measurements

**Grade 2**
- *Literature:* A Christmas Carol, "The Emperor's New Clothes," Native American stories of Iktomi, Peter Pan, Robin Hood legend, Greek myths
- *World History:* Ancient Greece, Alexander the Great, the Great Wall of China
- *American History:* The War of 1812 and the "Star Spangled Banner," Lincoln, Harriet Tubman and the "Underground Railroad," Rosa Parks and Martin Luther King Jr.
- *Music:* kinds of musical instruments (percussion, strings, winds, keyboards, etc.)
- *Math:* two-digit addition and subtraction to 18, telling time to five minutes, simple multiplication
- *Science:* seasons and the life cycle, simple tools (plane, wedge, pulley)

**Grade 3**
- *Literature:* William Tell, "Ali Baba and the Forty Thieves," "The People Could Fly," Alice in Wonderland, Norse mythology, "Three Words of Wisdom"
- *World History:* ancient Rome, Hannibal, Constantine
- *American History:* Eastern Woodland tribes, Pocahontas, the Plymouth Colony
- *Art:** Mary Cassatt, Rembrandt
- *Math:* multiplying to 10 x 10, division
- *Science:* the food chain and the balance of nature, pollution, conservation, recycling, the speed of light.

*Although art first appears in this list at Grade 3, it is part of the Core Knowledge curriculum from kindergarten onward.

(continued on next page)

Figure 2.1.—*CONTINUED*

## Selected Topics from the Core Knowledge Curriculum

**Grade 4**
- *Literature:* Gulliver's voyage to Lilliput, *Robinson Crusoe*, Rip Van Winkle, legends of King Arthur, "The Fire on the Mountain," Sojourner Truth
- *Geography:* latitude, longitude, geography of Africa
- *World History:* the Middle Ages, King John and the Magna Carta, Kublai Khan and Marco Polo, African kingdoms, Islam
- *American History:* George Washington at Valley Forge, the Constitution and the Bill of Rights, forced removal of Native Americans, abolitionists, Sojourner Truth, women's rights
- *Art:* Gothic architecture
- *Music:* Haydn, Strauss
- *Math:* kinds of polygrams, fractions, decimals, volume
- *Science:* fossils, earthquakes and volcanoes, continental drift

**Grade 5**
- *Literature:* "A Midsummer Night's Dream," *Don Quixote*, *Tom Sawyer*, poems of Emily Dickinson and Langston Hughes, the Gettysburg Address
- *Geography:* climate zones and time zones
- *World History:* the "Age of Exploration," East African city-states, feudal Japan, the Renaissance, the English civil war
- *American History:* the Civil War, Reconstruction, Battle of the Little Big Horn, Homestead Act
- *Art:* Leonardo da Vinci's *The Last Supper* and *Mona Lisa*, Michelangelo's *David* and *Creation of Adam*
- *Math:* mixed numbers and fractions, rounding decimals, equations and variables, probability and statistics
- *Science:* phases of matter and transfer of energy

**Grade 6**
- *Literature:* *Pygmalion*, Orpheus and Eurydice, "Julius Caesar," *A Tale of Two Cities*, *The Secret Garden*, "Stopping by Woods on a Snowy Evening," poetry of Maya Angelou
- *World History:* Industrial Revolution, capitalism and socialism, the Enlightenment, Latin American independence

(continued on next page)

---

FIGURE 2.1.—*CONTINUED*

### SELECTED TOPICS FROM THE CORE KNOWLEDGE CURRICULUM

---

**Grade 6—continued**
- **American History:** immigration, the American Federation of Labor, William Jennings Bryan, W.E.B. DuBois, "The Souls of Black Folk," "Remember the Maine"
- **Music:** romantic composers, Berlioz
- **Art:** impressionism, Mathew Brady, Edward Degas
- **Math:** volume of rectangular solids, dividing decimals, reciprocals
- **Science:** genetics, chemical reactions, the electromagnetic spectrum

Note: As of the 1995 revision, the Core Knowledge curriculum includes kindergarten.

*Source:* Core Knowledge Foundation 1995.

---

to a gas and back again, and understand how this relates to clouds, fog, and precipitation." Activities for the teacher include "Introduce the different clouds and how they are formed," and for the student, "[I]llustrate the types of clouds by drawing on paper or using cotton balls to make formations."

The unit also includes a list of resources, sample assessments, readings, worksheets, and daily lesson plans on which objectives, standards, and activities are organized for each lesson in the unit.

### Teacher Attitudes About Core Knowledge

Hansberry teachers I spoke with had strong feelings about the Core Knowledge curriculum. One 1st grade teacher believed that these standards put his students on a par with students in Europe and Japan. He was glad not to be working with a "watered-down" curriculum. But another teacher felt that the Core Knowledge books did not include enough material about Latino culture. She regretted that many children at her school might not see themselves in their

FIGURE 2.2.

**MODERN RED SCHOOLHOUSE SELECTED PERFORMANCE STATEMENTS AND SAMPLE STANDARDS FOR THE PRIMARY LEVEL**

**English Language Arts**

*Performance Statement:* Each student can identify facts, place events in sequence, draw inferences, make judgments, and describe the details and content of a variety of literary and nonliterary texts, including narratives, stories, poetry, expository texts, articles, and instructions.

*Sample Standard:* Each student can draw from a reservoir of archetypal stories—including major myths, folk tales, and narratives from the United States and cultures worldwide—in order to describe conventional characters, plots, and themes; understand common allusions and metaphorical phrases; make predictions and relate experiences to his or her own life.

**Geography**

*Performance Statement:* Each student understands how spatial connections among people, places, and regions affect the movement of people, goods, and ideas.

*Sample Standard:* Each student can identify occupations and industries in different parts of own state and give geographical reasons for their presence.

**History**

*Performance Statement:* Each student can identify characteristics and accomplishments of major world civilizations in such places as Europe, Africa, the Americas, and Asia. Each student can show an understanding of how selected cultures are represented in the beliefs and practices of the United States and how they have helped to form a national heritage.

*Sample Standard:* Each student can show a basic understanding of North, Central, and South American, European, African, and Asian cultures as seen through their literature, customs, art, religion, and history by describing, for example, the form and purpose of such things as the Great Pyramids, the Roman roads, the Crusades, the English Parliament, the Great Wall, and the League of the Iroquois.

*(continued on next page)*

FIGURE 2.2.—*CONTINUED*

## MODERN RED SCHOOLHOUSE SELECTED PERFORMANCE STATEMENTS AND SAMPLE STANDARDS FOR THE PRIMARY LEVEL

### Science
*Performance Statement:* Each student can show an emerging understanding of the basic principles of physical sciences, particularly in relation to the six themes: energy, evolution, patterns of change, patterns of stability, scale and structure, systems and interactions.

*Sample Standard:* Each student can show a basic understanding of energy in light and heat, particularly as generated by the sun, understand that heat transfers from warmer objects to cooler, show that some materials conduct heat better than others, and explain how electric power can be conserved and why it should be.

### Mathematics
*Performance Statement:* Each student can solve real-world problems using knowledge of numbers, numeration, and basic mathematical operations.

*Sample Standard:* Each student can use mathematics as a way to understand other areas of the curriculum, for example, using measurement in science and computing the passage of time in history.

### Foreign Language
*Performance Statement:* Each student can communicate effectively and appropriately in the chosen language when confronted with a range of everyday situations.

*Sample Standard:* Given familiar everyday situations (such as family, school, friends, food, recreation, and one's individual needs), each student can make appropriate comments, initiate and respond to simple statements, and maintain simple face-to-face conversations.

### Health and Physical Education
*Performance Statement:* Personal Fitness: Each student can measure and analyze personal fitness, and participate in sports and/or recreational activities that promote health and physical fitness.

*Sample Standard:* Each student can demonstrate an understanding of the mechanical principles related to movement (e.g., throwing, running, catching) and perform movement skills effectively.

(continued on next page)

---

Figure 2.2.—*CONTINUED*

## Modern Red Schoolhouse Selected Performance Statements and Sample Standards for the Primary Level

---

### Visual Arts

*Performance Statement:* Each student can create with various art media to express ideas and experiences.

*Sample Standard:* Each student can design and create simple works of art using different media, techniques, and processes—such as drawing, painting, sculpture, printmaking, design, film, or video—that express an intended purpose.

### Music

*Performance Statement:* Each student shows skill in listening and responding to music, can identify certain features of music, and can offer ideas about the music's meaning and purpose.

*Sample Standard:* Each student can explain the effect of a composer's choices—such as the choice of instruments, key signature, and duration—and describe his or her response using appropriate music vocabulary—for example, melody, rhythm, harmony, tempo.

### Drama

*Performance Statement:* Each student understands the influence of drama in human life and can use past and present dramatizations of people's lives to explore connections among people and cultures.

*Sample Standard:* Each student can relate basic stories and specific scenes from a selection of exemplary dramatic works—for example, scenes from Shakespeare, or film and television scripts adapted from classic children's literature. Each student can identify the historical period and culture associated with the particular work.

*Source:* Hudson Institute, April 1995.

---

school's curriculum. To remedy the situation, she joined with others to infuse the curriculum with more Latino literature and folk tales. A member of the Core Knowledge Foundation explained to me that because their program is meant to take up 50 percent of the school program, this type of addition is a natural way to tailor the curriculum to meet local needs.

### The Individual Education Compact: Student Accountability

The Individual Education Compact (IEC) at Hansberry is an important assessment tool linking instruction and curriculum to student performance. Each student in a Modern Red Schoolhouse uses the IEC to track progress in meeting curriculum goals. This plan is an agreement among the student, the advising teacher, and the student's family, and it is reviewed regularly. With the IEC, the parties can determine how well the student is advancing, how teachers and family members can offer support, and what areas might require special help.

## SQUIRES: ACCOMMODATING A STATE CURRICULUM FRAMEWORK

For Jay Jordan and the teachers at Squires Elementary School in Lexington, Kentucky, curriculum leadership required working within the Kentucky Education Reform Act (KERA). This statewide comprehensive strategy to upgrade Kentucky's educational system affects all aspects of education, including governance, finance, curriculum, and assessment.

### KERA's Curriculum Goals

In the area of curriculum, Kentucky has adopted the following six Learning Goals (Kentucky Department of Education 1994), which describe the skills and abilities expected from high school graduates:

1. Students are able to use basic communication and math skills for purposes and situations similar to what they will encounter throughout their lives.
2. Students shall develop their abilities to apply core concepts and principles from mathematics, the sciences, the arts, the humanities, social studies, practical living studies, and vocational studies to situations and problems similar to what they will encounter throughout their lives.
3. Students shall develop their abilities to become self-sufficient individuals.
4. Students shall develop their abilities to become responsible members of a family, work groups, or community, including demonstrating effectiveness in community service.

5. Students shall develop their abilities to think and solve problems in school situations and in a variety of situations they will encounter in life.

6. Students shall develop their abilities to connect and integrate experiences and new knowledge from all subject matter fields with what they have previously learned and build on past learning experiences to acquire new information through various media sources.

Under each of these six Learning Goals are a series of Academic Expectations. For example, under Goal One, students are expected to "use reference tools such as dictionaries, almanacs, encyclopedias, and computer reference programs and research tools such as interviews and surveys to find the information they need to meet specific demands, explore interests, or solve problems." Students are also expected to "write using appropriate forms, conventions, and styles to communicate ideas and information to different audiences for different purposes." Communication also includes mathematics and the visual and performing arts.

Academic Expectations under Goal Two refer specifically to skills and knowledge in the academic disciplines of mathematics (for example, "understand various mathematical procedures and use them appropriately and accurately"), science (for example, "use the concept of scale and scientific models to explain the organization and functioning of living and nonliving things and predict other characteristics that might be observed"), arts and humanities (for example, "[have] knowledge of major works of art, music, and literature and appreciate creativity and the contributions of the arts and humanities"), social studies (for example, "can accurately describe various forms of government and analyze issues that relate to the rights and responsibilities of citizens in a democracy"), practical living (for example, "[have] the knowledge and skills they need to remain physically healthy and to accept responsibility for their own physical well-being"), and vocational studies (for example, "[have] skills such as interviewing, writing resumes, and completing applications that are needed to be accepted into college or other postsecondary training or to get a job").

Goals Three and Four are not included in the Kentucky assessment program and do not have specific Academic Expectations. Academic Expectations for Goal Five include "Students use creative thinking skills to develop or invent novel, constructive ideas or products." Finally, Academic Expectations under Goal Six include "Students expand their understanding of existing knowledge by making connections with new knowledge, skills, and experiences."

An accountability system is tied to these Learning Goals. The Kentucky Instructional Results Information System (KIRIS) includes a written test, performance events, and portfolio review in the areas of reading, writing, mathematics, science, and social studies. Performance events and written tests occur in grades 4, 8, and 11. Portfolio reviews take place in grades 5, 8, and 12, with student work rated as novice, apprentice, proficient, or distinguished. The accountability system results in a rating for each school, and schools are expected to meet improvement targets. This creates a high-stakes situation, because the system is tied to rewards and sanctions for the schools, and results are made public.

## KERA AND LOCAL CURRICULUM EFFORTS

Because the Kentucky Education Reform Act shifts much of the curriculum development responsibility from the district central office to the school, it is the responsibility of principals such as Jordan and their school communities to make local decisions that will help their students achieve results required under state law.

Squires Elementary made at least two important decisions regarding curriculum. First, the school decided to use the HELPS unit-planning strategy developed by the National Alliance for School Restructuring, thus taking advantage of an important affiliation that their school had developed. The HELPS process enables teachers to create standards-based units that include important culminating activities. Much of the responsibility for learning is placed on students, who must make numerous decisions and participate actively. The first schoolwide use of HELPS at Squires centered around an interdisciplinary unit culminating in the simulation of a mall in the school. Students had to learn how to design and market products and services, decide on budgets, sell stock, vie for the best locations, and compete for market share. Families came to the school when the mall experiment opened for business, and students had a chance to see how well their business plans might operate in the real world. Students, parents, and faculty reacted positively to the mall unit, and the school planned to repeat the idea of a schoolwide interdisciplinary unit.

The second decision made at Squires involved adopting the Different Way of Knowing (DWOK) curriculum developed at the Galef Institute in Los Angeles. Different Way of Knowing emphasizes strong, interdisciplinary content linking social studies to the arts, language arts, math, and science. The K–6 program also includes professional development training for teachers and administrators through seminars and summer institutes. During the 1995–96 school year, 376 schools in seven states serving 80,820 students were affiliated with DWOK; 62,100 of these students were in Kentucky (Galef Institute 1996).

## THE DWOK CURRICULUM

The DWOK curriculum is organized around six large modules:

- Families: Caring for One Another (primary grades)
- America's Family Stories (primary-elementary grades)
- Community Problem Solving: Water, Air, Garbage (primary-elementary grades)
- A Geography Journey: Adventuring in the U.S. (elementary-upper grades)
- Choices, Chance, and Change: America's Story to 1776 (upper elementary-middle school)
- History Mysteries: Discovering the Past (upper elementary-middle schools)

Each of the modules has four stages, called "Wheels." Wheel One is titled "Exploring What You Already Know." At this stage, students discover how their own background knowledge connects with the new topic. Wheel Two is "Getting Smarter Through Research." Here, students engage in what are called "clusters." Through clusters, students gain content knowledge through hands-on activities, such as creating models and role playing. Wheel Three, "Becoming an Expert," allows students to work individually and in groups to apply their knowledge through in-depth projects. During Wheel Four, "Making Connections," students extend their learning by reaching others in and beyond their school and by engaging their families.

The upper-elementary module "A Geography Journey: Adventuring in the U.S." provides an example of how the DWOK curriculum works in practice. Knowledge goals for this module include the following:

- The United States is characterized by a diversity of geographic features, including oceans, mountains, forests, rivers and lakes, and deserts.
- The United States can be divided into regions—by location, physical features, climate, wildlife, and vegetation.
- Places are special to different people for different reasons.

In Wheel One ("Exploring What You Already Know"), students determine what they already know about exploring places. They reflect on places they experience in everyday settings. They use their senses to explore the outdoors as well. In Wheel Two ("Getting Smarter Through Research"), students pose questions such as, "What do we want to know about oceans, mountains, forests, rivers and lakes, or deserts?" This module features a "Getting Started" project, followed by five clusters. In the "Getting Started" section, students meet two fictitious characters and pretend to travel with them as they make field guide kits that they will use to collect the work they produce in the rest of the module. The clusters that follow are "Exploring the Ocean," "Exploring the Mountains," "Exploring the Forests," "Exploring Rivers and Lakes," and "Exploring the Desert." In the clusters, students read works such as Ruth Yaffe Radin's *High in the Mountains*. They create storyboards of adventures, form and test hypotheses, study related artwork, and study such central concepts as the desert water cycle.

At the conclusion of Wheel Two, students demonstrate their learning through projects including multimedia maps. This leads to Wheel Three ("Becoming an Expert"), during which students ask,

"What are some of the adventures I could have in different parts of the United States?" They use a mapping game to demonstrate general knowledge, and they prepare to focus on one particular part of U.S. geography of most interest to them. The final Wheel ("Making Connections") poses the question, "How can we use what we've learned about the physical geography of the United States?" Students find ways to "connect" what they've learned to their own lives and start planning for their next area of learning.

The curriculum guide follows with a list of what are called "Learning Opportunities" (for example, making field guide kits, creating multimedia maps, writing journals, writing postcards from amazing places), mini-lessons (for example, planning a presentation, role-playing drama and movement techniques, understanding scale, keeping a bibliography), and interdisciplinary connections (for example, connections to writing, science, history, "your state," visual arts, movement and dance, math, music, and drama). The guide concludes with lists of related literature and supporting instructional material.

DWOK's approach starts with an inventory of the knowledge that students bring to the subject and continues by encouraging students to create and organize a variety of products and demonstrations that show progress toward learning goals. In this way, assessment is interwoven with instruction.

Like their colleagues at Three Oaks and Hansberry, teachers at Squires feared unintended gaps and overlaps in their curriculum. Because of its predictable sequence of modules, their chosen program helped them avoid these pitfalls. Teachers also were pleased with the increase in depth of learning their students experienced. When one 5th grade class studied the module "Choice, Chance and Change: America's Story to 1776," students agreed to create a museum on Native Americans. Children selected a tribe and focused on such aspects as communication, art, music, and dance. Teachers acted as guides for the museum while students researched, planned, and constructed the exhibitions. One teacher, who is also the mother of a student in this class, said that the museum project followed them wherever they went. Her daughter organized a shopping trip to purchase walnut dyes for her dress so that it could be made in an authentic way.

Whether using the Core Knowledge curriculum to organize learning for a thousand students in southern Florida, joining the Modern Red Schoolhouse project to coordinate curriculum with other central aspects of learning for hundreds of children in the Bronx, or using Different Way of Knowing to provide an interdisciplinary learning program that connects to state requirements in Kentucky, adopters made thoughtful decisions for their schools. These selections required staff agreement and a great deal of learning for everyone. Adopting, like the two other curriculum options, is an active process that needs time to reach maturity.

Teachers in the adopting group did not consider this option to be an uninspiring choice. They spoke glowingly of their creative work and felt that there was much room for them and for their students to add their own touch to the various curriculum plans. But what kind of creativity might schools exercise when states or districts present very specific guidelines—requirements that are not written as exit qualities or frameworks but are grade-level specific and highly detailed? Next we will turn to the case of the evolvers, who faced just this situation.

## The Evolvers

A key issue for the two evolver sites, Burruss and Sinclair, was their starting points. Each was required to work within well-defined boundaries. Both found ways to use the boundaries to encourage curriculum development. In an interesting twist of the normal complaints about imposed guidelines, these schools saw the guidelines as liberating because they provided an agreed upon framework. The guidelines also illustrate the curriculum-instruction-assessment relationship described in Chapter 1. Leaders at these schools understood where their freedom to operate was located, and they started there.

### BURRUSS: USING STATE GUIDELINES TO SHAPE CHANGE

Jerry Locke and his staff at Burruss Elementary School set out for new curricular directions, but they had to start with their state's mandated curriculum. The Georgia Quality Core Curriculum articulates standards in the following areas:

- Language arts (literature, reading, listening, speaking, writing, reference and study skills)
- Mathematics (numeration, operations, problem solving, measurement, geometry, probability and statistics, fractions, decimals)
- Science (process skills, physical science, life science, earth science, environment, science, technology and society, reference skills)
- Social studies (key topics such as families, communities, culture and geographic regions, colonial history of the United States, locating, analyzing, and evaluating data, map and globe skills, problem-solving skills, social participation skills, time and chronology)
- Physical education (physical fitness, movement)
- Health (safety, nutrition, personal health)
- Art (perceptual awareness, production of artwork, artistic heritage, art criticism, aesthetic judgment)
- Music (listening skills, performance skills, creative skills, knowledge and understanding, attitudes and appreciations)

The standards of the Quality Core Curriculum are fairly specific. For example, here are some of the things that a 3rd grade student is expected to do:

- Language arts (literature/reading): Recognizes main ideas, details, sequence of events, and cause-effect relationships.
- Mathematics (operations): Determines basic multiplication and division facts through 9 x 9 by using strategies such as skip counting, multiplying by zero and one, dividing by one, splitting rays, commutative property of multiplication, using known facts to find unknown facts.
- Science (earth science): Investigates weather phenomena and makes observations using weather-related instruments.
- Physical education (physical fitness): Demonstrates correct stretching techniques, such as reachers, and holds stretch 15–45 seconds, breathes continuously and does not bounce.
- Health (safety): Identifies appropriate first-aid procedures for common injuries.

- Art (production of artwork): Creates artwork that demonstrates an awareness of details observed in the environment.

Somewhat surprisingly, many Burruss teachers react to this state-mandated curriculum with something close to gratitude. Many offered remarks such as, "It gives us an idea of what we must attend to." I was reminded of a poet's lecture on her love of writing sonnets. She said that it was like filling a glass bottle with layers of colored sand. Once you accepted the contours of the bottle, you could concentrate on the freedom you had in organizing the sand in beautiful layers. In much the same way, the Georgia Quality Core Curriculum provides the general shape of content, giving teachers room to be creative in delivering it.

Instead of discussing what to teach in which grades, teachers offered creative instructional ideas such as the SUCCESS program for literacy. This K–5 reading and writing program focuses on four components taught daily: word study (phonics and spelling), research (finding information, organizing data, and presenting findings), writing (daily creative and high-interest writing), and recreational reading (free reading in a relaxed atmosphere). By starting with instruction, Burruss took advantage of an area of freedom; the state does require certain content, but method is left up to the school.

From Chapter 1 we know, however, that when one part of the curriculum-instruction-assessment triangle is pulled, the other two elements are affected. One way to see the SUCCESS program is as an instructional issue. Another aspect of it is the large amount of quality literature that children are exposed to from their first days of school. That literature represents a curricular change, just as measuring the degree of children's understanding is an assessment issue.

Burruss teachers and administrators have made the SUCCESS program a normal part of their work, and that has led to other innovations. Interdisciplinary studies have become part of accepted practice at the school, as have a wide range of extracurricular academic programs. The extracurricular programs are the result of a strong partnership between staff and Burruss's PTA. They include Math Super Sleuths (a problem-solving enrichment program), Junior Great Books, the Writer's Guild (a program that allows children to share their favorite writing with others), the Literary Guild (a program that recognizes students for reading extensively), Odyssey of the Mind (a program that brings students together for creative group problem solving), Choir, Chess Club, Explora Vision (a program in which students design commercial products for the future), and Beaver Publishing (which publishes children's books). Many of these programs occur during the school day and exemplify how Burruss extends and develops the curriculum the state requires.

### Sinclair: Finding Flexibility in the Provincial Curriculum

Just as the Georgia Quality Core Curriculum defined much of Burruss's curriculum, the Ontario Common Curriculum for grades 1–9 (Ontario Ministry for Education and Training 1993) helped to define expectations for 9th grade students at the Sinclair Secondary School. The Common Curriculum is built upon four principles:

- Learning (For example, "Learning involves developing values as well as knowledge and skills.")
- Teaching (For example, "Integrated teaching methods are best developed through discussion and experimentation involving all members of the school community.")
- Curriculum (For example, "An integrated curriculum is necessary to prepare students for the modern world.")
- Assessment (For example, "Teachers need to use a wide variety of appropriate assessment methods.")

These principles lead to 10 Learning Outcomes expected of all students by the end of 9th grade. Students are expected to do the following:

- Be able to use language to think, learn, and communicate effectively.
- Be able to use mathematical knowledge and skills effectively.
- Be able to apply scientific methods and knowledge in understanding the world, solving problems, and making responsible decisions.
- Be able to use a wide variety of technologies effectively.
- Be able to apply historical and geographical knowledge

in analyzing world events and understanding different cultures.

- Show a commitment to peace, social justice, and the protection of the environment in their own community, Canada, and the world.
- Have the skills needed to get along well with other people, show respect for human rights, and practice responsible citizenship.
- Find satisfaction and purpose in work and learning, and plan properly for entering the work force or continuing their education.
- Appreciate, enjoy, and participate in the arts.
- Build healthy lifestyles and relationships.

These outcomes are approached through four core program areas:

- Language
- The Arts
- Self and Society
- Mathematics, Science, and Technology

To meet the requirements of the Common Curriculum in its own way, Sinclair created an untracked, interdisciplinary 9th grade program. Students work in four broad fields:

- The Arts (music, art, drama, dance)
- Communications in a Global World (English, French, geography)
- Mathematics-Science-Technology
- Skills for Living (business, family studies, physical and health education)

The first three are each designed to be taught as coordinated packages balancing discipline skills with a sense of the development of the whole field. For example, in the integrated arts package, students decide which of the arts (art, instrumental music, keyboards, vocal music, drama) they want to concentrate in. On Monday and Friday they receive 70 minutes of instruction in those areas. On Tuesdays and Thursdays, the arts are combined for 95-minute blocks that cover one theme per semester. Themes have included "Medieval Arts" and "Rhythm and Movement in Modern Arts."

The Communications program, like the Math-Science-Technology program, occupies half of the school day, usually the afternoon. Students spend one-half year in each program, switching at midpoint. The three integrated subjects of Communications—English, French, and geography—share common themes. Themes have included "New Beginnings" (orienting to high school, exploring origins, the study of heroes and orienting around the globe); "Community" (stereotyping; study in French of what our community has to offer visitors; refugee status and quotas); "Issues" (creative controversy; expressing ideas, opinions, emotions, attitudes in French; and environmental issues at local, regional, provincial, and national levels); "Survival" (survival tactics in the wilderness; French vocabulary for wilderness and survival tactics; vegetation of various regions); and "The Future" (careers of the future; making predictions in French; Toronto 2010 and beyond in the areas of transportation, ethnic diversity, and population; changes in industry, energy consumption, and conservation).

The integrated Math-Science-Technology (MST) program works in a similar fashion, using themes to link the three disciplines. Themes have included "Lighten-Up" (graphing, reflections, light, mirrors, light meters, cameras); "Mystery and Magic" (variables and polynomials, atoms and molecules, crystal structure models); "Co-Motion" (statistics, graphing experiments, design projects such as hot air balloons); and "Green Thumb" (volume/perimeter of gardens and flower beds, landscaping, designing a landscaped yard).

Besides the integrated themes, MST has a four-week period referred to as "Dis-Integration" time. This month of study allows each of the three disciplines to attend to important material that is content specific to that field. Science uses its time to work on such things as measuring skills; mathematics attends to the format for problem solving; and technology teaches students about shop safety and the use of power hand tools.

In both Communications and MST, some groups of students work with a team of teachers, and others meet with one teacher. Students working with separate teachers go to each teacher every afternoon. Students with one teacher meet with that teacher for expanded blocks of time. Teachers reported advantages to each format, as well as some challenges. A single teacher working in Communications, for instance, must be able to teach French. Consequently, the role often falls to the French teachers. Similarly, in MST, teachers of science or mathematics need to understand technology and fabrication techniques.

Because the Ontario Ministry of Education and Training has more specific course requirements for upper high school grades, Sinclair has concentrated most of its subject integration in the 9th grade. In the upper grades, Canadian Studies combines 10th grade English with social studies. The Senior Outdoor Pursuits Course connects environmental geography with physical education. Although Sinclair is not unique in these offerings, they do show continuity with the 9th grade pattern.

By thinking about time in a more flexible way, teachers and administrators at Sinclair have extended the spirit of the integrated 9th grade to all students by making Wednesday a day for exploration and extended study. Students sign up in advance for curricular and extracurricular projects in a wide range of subjects and fields. Some use this time for extra help in subjects such as math or foreign language, while others use the day to delve into important social issues such as sexual harassment. Some students explore new art forms such as calligraphy, and others find that such opportunities as an art/history trip focusing on the 1920s meet their needs and interests. One student I spoke with took an introductory course on flying. For all Sinclair students, Wednesday is a day to discover new fields and work with students from every grade.

However interesting these curriculum innovations appear, the integrated 9th grade program and the Wednesday directed study schedule did not evolve without controversy. Criticism came from teachers in other schools in the district, as well as from concerned parents who wondered whether their children were receiving sufficient depth of knowledge in the disciplines. During the first year of implementation, 400 people came to an emotional meeting about the 9th grade curriculum. At that session, school leaders described the provincial Common Curriculum and presented related reasons why this approach was taken. In the end a few families did leave the school, but the vast majority stayed. Similar communication with parents helped them understand the Wednesday program, and parental feedback gave teachers ideas for improvements. As a result of increasing community awareness of its programs and the faculty's responsiveness to new ideas, the second annual curriculum night drew only 100 parents and was far calmer.

Some settings face a different situation than the adopters and the evolvers. These settings have a strong tradition of local control, and curriculum leaders at these schools and districts must find ways to move their curriculum plans with a minimum of outside direction. These are the developers.

## The Developers

The developers spent a great deal of time inventing their whole program on site. While all public schools must respond to higher authorities at the district and state level, the relative freedom these sites enjoyed enabled them to create their programs with few restrictions. Unlike the adopters, these schools did not focus on one program that met most of their curricular needs. Instead, their educational programs are the result of continuous discussion among teachers, administrators, students, parents, and community members. Developers, like adopters and evolvers, do not see their learning program as a finished product. The following accounts simply describe the current state of their work.

### CABOT: BUILDING A STANDARDS-BASED CURRICULUM

The Cabot School has had considerable freedom to plan its own curriculum direction. The state of Vermont has no mandated curriculum, although in 1993 the state board adopted the Vermont Common Core (Gross 1996). The Common Core describes four areas of Vital Results:

- Communications
- Reasoning and Problem Solving
- Personal Development
- Social Responsibility

Vermont also requires a portfolio assessment in writing and mathematics during upper elementary and middle grades. Beyond this, local districts are expected to create their own curriculum. Vermont now has a Framework designed to guide curriculum development at the local level. As described in Chapter 1, Cabot's curriculum development originated with a planning group composed of community members and faculty. This group's work resulted in 12 graduation requirements:

> Beginning with the Class of 1998, each graduate:
>
> 1. Will be able to appreciate the arts and the value of competent craftsmanship.
> 2. Will be able to read for comprehension and enjoyment.
> 3. Will be able to write and speak clearly and effectively.
> 4. Will be able to read, write, speak and comprehend another language.
> 5. Will be able to compute and interpret numbers.
> 6. Will be able to formulate concepts, gather and interpret data, apply problem-solving skills, and reach reasoned conclusions.
> 7. Will be aware of scientific discovery and advances and their social impact.
> 8. Will be able to use a variety of current technology.
> 9. Will be aware of the inter-relatedness of all disciplines (science, math, social science, literature, languages, and the arts).
> 10. Will be prepared to function as an informed and interested citizen.
> 11. Will be able to manage him/herself in the American economic system.
> 12. Will be prepared to function as a socially responsible, healthy, physically fit, and independent individual.

From these 12 requirements, the school community has created benchmarks that define standards, places where evidence of achievement may be collected, and instructional guidelines. In addition, the school has grade-level benchmarks for kindergarten and 2nd, 4th, 6th, 8th, and 10th grades. This allows teachers, administrators, students, and their parents to track the development of skills and knowledge throughout the course of the student's time at the school.

Here is an example of how Cabot's program works. The second graduation requirement says that graduates will be able to read for comprehension and enjoyment. Related Graduation Standards include such questions as, "Has the student read examples of excellent writing?" and "Can s/he understand and discuss a wide variety of written work (scientific, technical, analytical, narrative, expressive, and imaginative)?" Evidence that may answer these questions may be found in the student's humanities portfolio (where an "analysis of a character in a novel or a play" may be kept) or in the research component of the Senior Thesis. Instructional guidelines for grades 11 and 12 include "reading of the student's choice in the curriculum; time for reading during every school day; regular time for sharing/discussing what's read; active participation in senior book discussion group; exposure to finest examples of a variety of literary forms." Similar guidelines in this and all other fields begin at the kindergarten level and grow with students as they advance through Cabot's program.

Cabot's experience clearly illustrates the curriculum-instruction-assessment triangle. Cabot started by setting standards for graduation. The term *standards-driven* is commonly used by people familiar with Cabot, illustrating how that agenda-setting curricular point of the triangle was pulled first. What remained to be defined were issues of how instruction would have to change to meet the requirements and how assessment could be defined to measure whether or not students reached the prescribed levels of achievement. The fact that Cabot's benchmarks are written in terms of standards, evidence, and instructional guidelines shows how easy it is to find elements of instruction and assessment in a curriculum document.

As might be expected, the Cabot community has worked hard to develop the two key areas of instruction and assessment. By the time Marge Sable left the school in 1994, 17 project teams, run by teachers, were underway. Some dealt with assessment issues such as a new report card that would better reflect new priorities. The entire faculty took a course on assessment in the fall of 1995 to start the process of completing that part of the triangle. But, as one science teacher told me, large questions still exist. Are the standards clear enough? Are there multiple ways of achieving them? What happens if a student cannot achieve the standards at all? Clearly this teacher was not afraid to hold her school up to some very tough standards.

Instruction has changed, too. Literacy education in the early grades has changed from a reliance on basal readers to multi-age instruction using programs such as Reading Recovery. Early years include a good deal of attention to language arts and mathematics skills, and teachers reported that students were reaching higher levels of performance. Aiding the changing instructional strategy and the push for higher standards is a commitment from the school board to support smaller class sizes. The goal is to have 15 students per teacher. Instruction in the middle grades also reflects multi-age instruction and a good deal of hands-on work. In one class students in the 5th and 6th grade researched an animal of their choice and created a drawing of the animal along with a description of that animal's special abilities. Teachers consulted with students during their work and gave them specific feedback as they progressed through the assignment. Although students had considerable range in choosing an animal, they all had to respond to the same standard of quality. Students had also studied human-made structures, such as buildings and moving vehicles, before their study of nature's creations. Speaking with them revealed that they understood that machinery could work much like animal anatomy. The movement of legs, for instance, could be similar to the movement initiated by the steering wheel of a car.

The senior high school was equally engaged in changing the learning program to meet the new requirements. One high school social studies class had become so expert in local history that they were able to dress in period costume and conduct tours of their community during fall foliage season. Proceeds from the tours went toward restoration of local historical sites. The social studies teacher also introduced a senior project program to Cabot. The program, known as IOTA, began as a voluntary effort but will be required of students who graduate beginning in 1998. IOTA students write a research project based on an original hypothesis, serve an internship, job shadow, perform community service, and present all of their work to a committee made up of peers, community members, and faculty. IOTA topics have included the therapeutic value of pets, the relationship of sign language to later language acquisition, medieval weapons and their design, and how an integrated arts program can promote children's learning.

### OCEANA: CENTERING RESPONSIBILITY ON THE LEARNER

Whereas Cabot's curriculum planning started before Vermont's voluntary curriculum guidelines existed, planners at Oceana needed to fit their work into three sets of existing expectations: the California frameworks in the academic disciplines, local district curriculum goals, and the University of California's requirements. Although this may sound formidable, none of the teachers, administrators, or community members interviewed complained about the need to meet the requirements of agencies beyond the school.

Oceana's curriculum rests on five Outcome Statements written by staff, students, parents, and businesspeople. Graduates are expected to be

- Proficient in basic skills of communication (reading, writing, listening, and speaking), mathematics, and physical fitness.
- Problem solvers who know how to visualize solutions, find resources, use technology, learn new skills, and follow a process.
- Creative, reflective, and critical thinkers who can express themselves, make reasoned judgments, defend choices, and interpret historical, scientific, artistic, and other evidence to help draw conclusions and help make life meaningful.
- Able to work independently and with others cooperatively to accomplish tasks that require planning, responsibility, presentation skills, and self-evaluation.
- Respectful of themselves, other people and cultures, the community, democratic values, and the environment.

Oceana's philosophy statement shows how these outcomes operate together:

> Each student will be expected to master essential skills and areas of knowledge. While these skills and areas will, to varying degrees, reflect the traditional academic disciplines, our

program's design will be shaped by the intellectual and imaginative powers and competencies that students need.

- Teaching and learning will be personalized.
- The student will be the worker, rather than the receiver of teacher-delivered instructional services.
- The diploma will be awarded upon exhibition by the student of his or her grasp of the central skills and knowledge of the school's program. The emphasis is on the students' demonstration that they have mastered important concepts and tasks.

### THE INTEGRATED HUMANITIES PROGRAM

One of the strongest examples of the restructured curriculum is the required four-year Humanities program, which uses annual themes to link social science, English, and fine arts. Members of the three departments created the program after studying the California Framework for English and Social Studies, examining the newest instructional materials, and reflecting on Oceana's guiding philosophy. At the 9th grade level, the program includes integrated projects from math and science. Humanities themes follow this pattern:

- Grade 9: "When Do We Grow Up?"—Dealing with coming of age in Inuit, Australian Aboriginal, African, Mexican, and Chinese cultures.
- Grade 10: "How Is the War Within Related to the War Without?"—Dealing with fascism, communism, nationalism, and "other problems of the modern world such as institutionalized racism."
- Grade 11: "Is the American Dream Myth or Reality?"—Using the theme of the American Dream to study political and social history, and literature from the American Revolution to the present.
- Grade 12 (Semester I): "What Is Power?"—Examining questions of governmental power and individual rights.
- Grade 12 (Semester II): "What Can You Expect When You Make a Journey?"—Considering what a life journey can be like, the way communities handle crises, and the content of life's decisions.

The spirit of interconnectedness in the Humanities was clearly evident when I observed a lesson conducted by a student teacher. The class first viewed a short video depicting architecture in Nazi Germany. Students then worked in cooperative groups to discuss the buildings they had just seen and to consider how they would feel living in such an environment, what the purpose of such architecture might be, and how art and politics relate to one another. Students took these questions very seriously and tried hard to imagine themselves in this situation. Finally, the groups designed their own cities on large posters. What was the underlying message of their city? How did shape, color, and size contribute to that message?

Two qualities of Oceana became clear as the students approached their assignment. First, they were accustomed to working in teams over extended periods of time. Second, they were very comfortable interpreting art and using art to express complex and abstract ideas. The normal boundaries between disciplines that exist for many students were nowhere apparent, nor did the students express the usual reticence that many adolescents show when asked to produce artwork. This lesson seemed to capture the ideal of an integrated approach. While the three departments involved in the Humanities program have combined their disciplines most thoroughly, others, such as the science department, are working toward the same ends.

The arts play a central role at Oceana. Oceana's art teacher has become an expert in integrating projects into the Humanities units of study, helping to bring various topics to life and reaching students at a different level through lessons on such things as the art of cave paintings or the making of Filipino masks. Working with a colleague in the mathematics department, she also designs projects that connect science and math to the Humanities program. When students made their own Chinese kites, for example, they designed their models in science class using calculations from their study of physics.

## COMMUNITY SERVICE AND INTERIM COURSES

Community service, Interim Courses, and the Senior Exhibition are as important as course content because Oceana's philosophy is so related to the student as worker. These elements represent opportunities for independent action and mature judgment.

Oceana expects each student to perform 100 hours of community service, normally distributed across all four years. The program is intended to bring students in direct contact with area residents and agencies, help students understand the role of volunteers in our society, see how academic skills can be applied, explore possible career options, and, according to the school's Parent Handbook, "promote maturity, self-reliance, decision making, problem solving, and self-esteem." Through the community service program, students work (under supervision) with young children, senior citizens, and homeless people, among others, in the Bay area. Students do all of their volunteer work outside of class time and must keep written records of their work. As we will see in Chapter 4, the power of having hundreds of students working with community residents over thousands of hours proved to be a crucial help when Oceana faced its period of crisis.

The Interim Course is another way in which Oceana promotes curricular diversity and student decision making. Like the Wednesday program at Sinclair, Oceana's Interim Course allows students to try out new ideas that may be academic (Oceanography, Photography, Arizona Science and Society), recreational (Hiking in the Bay Area, Foods, Boat Building), or vocational (Visiting Bay Area Colleges, Job Shadowing in Government, Aviation Career Opportunities) in emphasis. Students earn up to five units of credit during Interim, and courses last one week. How students plan for their Interim experience depends on their interests and the direction they have set for themselves.

### Senior Exhibition and Graduation Portfolios

The concept of student as worker is most evident in the Senior Exhibition and Graduation Portfolio, because these provide the opportunity for students to demonstrate their attainment of Oceana's educational outcomes. As described in the Parent Handbook, the portfolio includes "transcripts, attendance records, education plan/reflections on learning, postgraduation plan, service learning journal and reflection, autobiography, record of accomplishments, awards, extracurricular activities, resume, and evidence of achievement outcomes."

The Senior Exhibition is a work of original research that must include economic, political, and social issues. It is meant to take most of the senior year to complete and involves formulation of a question; research; a preliminary paper; work with a mentor; development of a visual, dramatic, or musical aid created by the student; and a formal presentation. Students' work is scored on a rubric that considers seven key areas. The areas and the criteria for a perfect score (three points) in each area are as follows:

- Introduction—Clearly and powerfully introduces the presentation and essential question.
- Exploration of Essential Question—Essential question has been explored from the point of view of several disciplines, including economics.
- Visual Aids—Visual aids are incorporated into exhibition and are necessary to convey evidence and data.
- Evidence—Many sources are cited to support more than one side of the essential question.
- Position on the Essential Question—Position on essential question has been defended using the strongest evidence.
- Conclusion—Powerfully states and defends position on essential question.
- Presentation—The 30-minute to 45-minute exhibition contains a variety of presentation skills, including 9 or 10 of the following: good pronunciation, good enunciation, proper tone, a variety of pitch and inflection, good poise, good posture, proper appearance, consistent eye contact, good volume and projection, proper pace and tempo.

A student receiving a perfect score in each area would have a total score of 21 points. Students must score at least one point in each area and a minimum of seven points to pass the exhibition.

Like Cabot's IOTA senior project, Oceana's Senior Exhibition and Graduation Portfolio connect curriculum changes and assessment. Both schools are phasing in a system of student-created proof of mastery. These new assessments are meant to help the students focus on their learning as whole cloth woven carefully over time, representing a very different view of the curriculum than either school had offered before its development in curriculum leadership.

By now you may have seen a strong pattern emerging. Curriculum leadership is flexible and can be shaped to meet many varied conditions. This helps explain the differing strategies leaders use to move their schools. What may be less clear is why the various plans seem to emphasize different content. To start to fill in this piece of the curriculum leadership puzzle, we will now examine relevant underlying belief systems.

## Four Belief Systems That Guide Curriculum Choices

One way to think about the curriculum plans of the schools is to consider their origins: from outside of the school, through an evolution of state mandates, or through local development. It is important to understand the curriculum plans from a second perspective as well: their underlying philosophies, or belief systems. The noted theologian Abraham Joshua Heschel (1955, p. 4) tells us, "Philosophy may be defined as the art of asking the right questions." In our case, the "right question" is, "What should the learning agenda be and how should it be organized?" In numerous interviews it became obvious that selections of content, methods, and even forms of assessment all flowed from strong personal and shared beliefs about the purpose of education in our society. While a detailed discussion of educational philosophy is beyond the limits of this book, it is useful to see where these schools stand in relation to four major systems of educational belief: essentialism, perennialism, progressivism, and existentialism (Glickman 1985). Figure 2.3 synthesizes some of the basic features of these four belief systems, and Figure 2.4 shows where the philosophies fall in terms of who controls the learning environment—adults or students—and who designs the curriculum—external sources or students. The following sections provide a sketch of the major ideas that each philosophy embodies.

### ESSENTIALISM

William Bagley, professor of education at Teachers College during the 1920s, described the main features of essentialism in this way

(Bagley 1926, 1964):

1. Young people need and deserve to have leadership in their education by adults.
2. Specific programs of study agreed to by grade level need to be devised. Too much curriculum is designed locally, resulting in too much variety serving little purpose. In a mobile society, this is especially problematic.
3. America's democracy is at risk; a rigorous education with high standards is essential. Standards must be held high for everyone, but individuals will need different amounts of time to reach those standards. Everyone must be rigorously disciplined to their responsibilities and made clearly aware of the pitfalls that await the spend thrift and the idler.
4. Elementary schools, especially, need structure. Vague subjects like social studies are of little value.
5. Too much leveling downward has taken place. We have moved away from "exacting studies" like Latin, Algebra, and Geometry.
6. The curriculum needs to be organized around logical, chronological, and causal relationships.
7. Too much reliance has been placed on projects and activities generated from the learner as a way of getting to important curriculum.

### PERENNIALISM

Robert Maynard Hutchins's writings (1964) on the perennial ideals of education have six key themes:

1. There is a difference between good and bad. Everything is not relative.
2. Good moral and intellectual habits are essential for development.
3. Social participation is required for democracy to work.
4. Education's aim is the improvement of people—to know the good.
5. The education which best fits free people is a liberal education. The origin of the very term liberal education refers to one free to pursue higher thoughts.

FIGURE 2.3.

## CHARACTERISTICS OF FOUR PHILOSOPHIES THAT GUIDE CURRICULUM LEADERSHIP

### ESSENTIALISM

Major elements:

- Structure and rigor
- Logical, chronological curriculum
- Emphasis on math and science

Goal: Protect democracy from foreign economic or political threat.

### PERENNIALISM

Major elements:

- Universal truths
- Moral and intellectual habits
- Emphasis on liberal arts for all

Goal: Nurture and regenerate democratic habits of mind.

### PROGRESSIVISM

Major elements:

- Respect for individuals
- Investigation/problem solving
- Emphasis on community standards

Goal: Build democracy through experience.

### EXISTENTIALISM

Major elements:

- Individual quest for meaning
- Self-structured learning
- Emphasis on one's own standards

Goal: Redefine democracy in personal terms.

6. Liberal education means exposure to classics of culture and science for everyone.

The classic 1892 Committee of Ten report shows just how seriously perennialists take the concept of sharing this liberal education with everyone: "Every subject that is taught at all in a secondary school should be taught in the same way and to the same extent to every pupil so long as he pursues it, no matter what the probable destination of the pupil may be—or at what point his education is to cease" (U.S. Bureau of Education 1893).

## EXISTENTIALISM

Existentialism, associated with the writer Albert Camus (1956) and others, describes the world in very different terms:

1. Life's complexities and diverse situations make a single code of behavior unlikely.
2. The fact that we all must face death creates a sense of absurdity in our struggles as well as a need to establish meaning in a personal way. We cannot completely know anyone besides ourselves, and our quest for meaning is an individual act.
3. Individuals must work out—for themselves—what is important and what values they will uphold. They must define for themselves what is worth knowing.
4. In education this means allowing students time and opportunity to define for themselves what matters and how to explore it. Student-directed learning exists today in what are called Democratic Schools, where the curriculum is not created and then delivered. The learning agenda comes from learners.

## PROGRESSIVISM

John Dewey, perhaps the person most associated with progressive education, described these four principles in his work *Democracy and Education* (1916):

1. Learning must be respectful of the learner's feelings and interests.
2. Investigation and problem solving are vital to learning.
3. Too much of children's learning relies on "second-hand and ready-made material."
4. Children must meet that which they study. They need to go outside, create lively classrooms, experiment in gardening, animals, cooking, sewing, music making. Learning must be hands on.

And so we see in the book Dewey coauthored with Evelyn

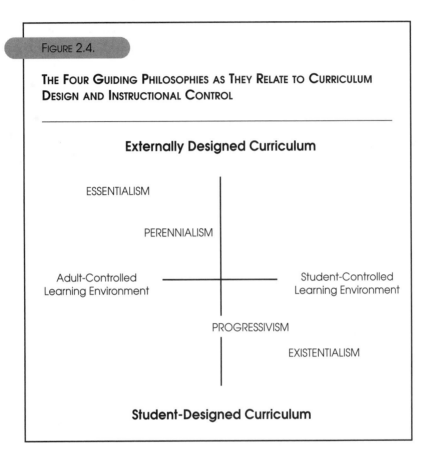

FIGURE 2.4.

**THE FOUR GUIDING PHILOSOPHIES AS THEY RELATE TO CURRICULUM DESIGN AND INSTRUCTIONAL CONTROL**

**Externally Designed Curriculum**

ESSENTIALISM

PERENNIALISM

Adult-Controlled
Learning Environment

Student-Controlled
Learning Environment

PROGRESSIVISM

EXISTENTIALISM

**Student-Designed Curriculum**

Dewey in 1915, entitled *Schools of Tomorrow*, photographs of industrial arts classes, life-size models of grocery store counters in the classroom, crafts shops, student dramas as a way of understanding ancient history, and model towns on the playground.[3]

The well-known project method advocated by another progressive, William Kilpatrick, shows another example of this kind of thinking in action (Kleibard 1986). Believing that subject matter was "a means not an end," Kilpatrick advocated long-term projects in which learners would identify major problems or key issues to be

[3]See *Education on the Dalton Plan* (Parkhurst 1922) for an additional variation of schools inspired by progressivism.

investigated and conduct appropriate research. In this way, the content could be learned through exploration in a manner relevant to the student.

The distinctions among these four philosophies are important because they help explain how sincere people look at the problem of organizing the curriculum and come to very different conclusions. The difference is not really in how perceptive they are in understanding educational needs, but in how they see the world. At the extremes, one either accepts the basic premise of these ideas or not. These beliefs have existed in our culture for a long time and seem likely to continue. Yet, people and the organizations they create are complex. In the real world very little can be so neatly pigeon-holed.

## Selecting and Blending:
## How Philosophies Work in Real Schools

The strong humanities content of the Core Knowledge curriculum at Three Oaks and Hansberry certainly sounds like the perennial ideal. The curriculum's attention to sequencing of topics and the careful progression of study is reminiscent of essentialism. The senior projects at Oceana and Cabot resemble the investigations called for by the progressives, and the tremendous number of cocurricular enrichment opportunities at Burruss call to mind the existentialist's personal pursuit of growth. All of these positions reflect personal beliefs that are shared by the schools and their communities. However, although the schools do have a dominant philosophical position, they also incorporate other points of view. The four philosophies play more like strong themes in the symphony of the schools rather than solo performances. In this way, Core Knowledge schools combine the study of classics—a perennialist goal—with a great amount of hands-on activity—a progressive approach. Cabot and Oceana may subscribe to progressive ideas in many ways, but instruction is organized around rigorous standards that reflect the structures imagined by essentialists. All of the sites paid at least some attention to the humanities so important to perennialists, yet, they allow room for many personal decisions—a key for existentialists. One way to look at these overlaps in philosophy is by means of a Venn diagram (see Figure 2.5). Purists might be distressed that this kind of blending takes place. Others might conclude that attempting to integrate the strengths of these four traditions is the height of wisdom.

So far we have seen diverse approaches to curriculum development and a similar variety in the belief systems that lead to curricular choices. You may now wonder, do these schools approach any educational issue in a like way? Their response to the challenge and promise of technology provides one good example of similar action taken.

## The Special Role of Technology

Despite the differences in their underlying belief systems, the 10 sites shared common ground in at least one area: the thorough integration of technology throughout their systems. Several of the schools and districts in this study made technology a top priority in their curriculum leadership activities. A grant from Apple Computer enabled the Cabot School to greatly increase student use of laptops and larger units. Burruss teachers experimented with student-authored multimedia slide shows. Working in small groups over three days, 4th grade students gathered information about sea life and used presentation software to create and edit their work, which included sound. Use of technology is at the center of the Modern Red Schoolhouse program used by Hansberry Elementary. By using local area networks (LANs), teachers can share information, curriculum plans (such as Hudson Units of study), keep track of students' individual educational compacts, and communicate with others through e-mail.

Sinclair Secondary School was designed to showcase technology. The media center has a large number of multimedia computers that allow students to access information in flexible ways. Computers are prevalent in many classrooms, and students work with them in small groups to solve problems. Teachers can call up videos from the media center through the internal cable system, and even student attendance is computerized. This high-tech environment illustrates the school board's commitment to technology and supporting networks. In the Northeast Arkansas District at Paragould, computer technology and sophisticated television and radio equipment support

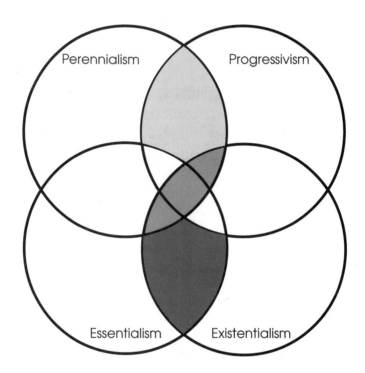

FIGURE 2.5.

## HOW THE PHILOSOPHIES OVERLAP AT THE SITES

The Core Knowledge approach at Three Oaks and Hansberry combines perennialist content with hands-on, progressivist instruction.

All sites emphasize the humanities, which can be seen as common ground of all four philosophies.

Oceana, Cabot, and Sinclair allow for many individual choices—an existentialist approach—but are organized around the rigorous standards favored by the essentialists.

curriculum goals. Students run their own television station, where school news and weather reports are taped, edited, and broadcast to the community over cable. Other students learn how to use ham radio to connect with people around the globe. Still others learn to use advanced equipment to measure such things as water quality so that the fish they raise in their aquaculture class will thrive. The Verona School District has developed a comprehensive plan to create a fiber optic network, improve the ratio of computers to students, establish standards for equipment purchases, access distance learning, and increase staff knowledge of technology.

Knowing the details of curriculum plans and something of how they came into being at the various sites is important information. But what are these places like in operation? What is life like for administrators, teachers, students, and their families? Finally, how is the spirit of curriculum leadership kept alive? To answer these questions, we will now examine how these schools have sustained curriculum leadership over time.

## Consider for a Moment

Before we go on, here are some questions that might help you apply the patterns of curriculum choices to your situation:

1. As you think about your school's situation and the requirements placed upon you, which path makes most sense: adopting, evolving, or developing?

2. As you look at the standards and curricular directions described in this chapter, which ones strike you as most interesting and important? Which ones do you want to learn more about?

3. Which philosophical tradition or combination best describes you, your colleagues, and your community? How does your philosophical position support your choice in Question 2?

# Sustaining Development: How Leaders Invent While They Implement Change

That philosophy which teaches us to follow in the beaten path, because it is most familiar, is erroneous; since its tendency is to put an end to all progress in knowledge.

—SALEM TOWN, *THE FOURTH READER*, 1849

Almost everyone has heard the lament about school restructuring: "They are expecting us to build a new airplane while we are flying the old one!" Too often, this remark is followed by despairing conversation about the futility of changing schools. The leaders are not perceived as serious. Or perhaps teachers are not given support for professional development and are not up to the job of serious change. Maybe it is a question of poor communication with the community. Finally, there are stories of children not ready for a more robust learning program.

The situation at the 10 sites described here is very different. Administrators are seen as crucial partners who uphold a vision for change that the school community subscribes to. Teachers are continuously learning, sharing in the job of governing the school, and exploring possible new directions. Parents and community groups make the schools a base of operations and have found roles that support the schools and push them further. Finally, students are responsible for their learning in new ways and seem to appreciate that shift.

None of these sites have completed their transition, as we will see in Chapter 4 when we consider the turbulence they have faced. However, they have been able to turn the idea of curriculum leadership from a promising possibility into a way of life. By sustaining development over time, they have been able to implement change while they invent new possibilities. Each stakeholder group—administrators, teachers, parents and community members, and students—plays a role in keeping these organizations moving. We'll look at each group in succession.

## The Administrators in Action

It is impossible to understand the story of curriculum leadership without analyzing the role of the site leaders themselves. In Chapter 1 we learned that these varied people shared similar personal qualities. We also learned of the central role they played in getting the process of change off the ground. Now we need to look at what these people do every day as they guide their schools and districts along the path of curriculum leadership. (Figure 3.1 outlines some key administrative activities.)

Understanding the leaders' role means understanding how they deal with four major challenges to their institutions. First, how do they develop a climate for sustained invention? Second, what key structures have they put into place to support curriculum change? Third, how have they developed and sustained positive relationships with governing bodies beyond the school, such as the district administration and board? Last, how have they anticipated and responded to the inevitable transitions that every system must face?

### DEVELOPING A CLIMATE FOR SUSTAINED INVENTION

Leaders and those with whom they work understand that their plans for curriculum change are for the long term. These plans require the organization to change its way of thinking about change itself. Continuous improvement is a hollow phrase, however, when the school is not set up to support all of the work implied in that concept. Early on these leaders established a cycle for inventing, testing, and evaluating new ideas in a way that fits their school or system. We have already seen the elements of this in Northeast Arkansas and Verona. These districts planned for support of new ideas in small settings. Then they gave the programs time to prove their worth. Finally, they evaluated the ideas and either shared them broadly or shelved them.

---

FIGURE 3.1.

**KEY ADMINISTRATIVE ACTIVITIES**

---

**Developing a Climate for Sustained Activity**
- Establish a cycle for inventing, testing, and evaluating new ideas
- Maintain a vigorous but reasonable pace for change
- Set realistic, attainable goals
- Stay close to the staff, parents, and community
- Hold the central vision

**Establishing Key Structures**
- Create shared governance mechanisms
- Seek support through regional and national affiliations
- Explore beyond the local area with staff
- Develop and share vital information about the school or district
- Create and support opportunities for ongoing professional development
- Develop positive relations with others in the school system and beyond

**Anticipating Transitions**
- Include new families in the vision
- Welcome new students and adjust conditions for them
- Respond to the needs of transient students
- Prepare the organization for the leader's departure

---

These steps are easy to state but hard to live by. In Arkansas, a highly transient student population, a relatively large staff, and student population growth were cited as barriers to making the system work easily. An influx of new students and new families also seems to be a complicating factor for other sites, especially Verona. Yet, having a plan for invention, maturation, and evaluation of ideas does provide a framework for thinking of change in a more developed and mature fashion.

Northeast Arkansas and Verona are not alone in emphasizing this dimension of leadership. Burruss's School Improvement Team is organized to make curriculum and related changes a central part of that school's shared governance, as we will soon see. The values guiding the Heron teachers' philosophy of inquiry, learning, local study, and networking also create a way of looking at change in a sustainable and developmental way. Another model for approaching change in a planned and thoughtful way is the detailed study that Oceana principal Lois Jones did of state law and current school hours when she petitioned her board for two hours each week for professional development.

Having a cycle of change in place is essential. But it is equally important to maintain a proper speed for change. Leaders of these sites grew in their understanding of just how many new projects a school can reasonably handle. At one point, Cabot, a very small school system, had 17 new projects. The system seemed tired, and the principal changed gears by emphasizing moderation. At Verona, this kind of understanding meant slowing down from the great speed with which a large and growing district was asking the public to assimilate new directions. In no sense did the leaders wither with the first complaint from a teacher or even a family. Rather, they had the maturity to evaluate the information they were receiving and consider objectively the system's ability to handle change.

The emphasis these people place on frankness also helped to create the feeling of openness that is so vital for continuous invention. All of the 10 leaders were clearly proud of their work and even more proud of the work of their colleagues and students. Yet, they all readily discussed how far they needed to go before they would be satisfied. They were objective in discussing the problems they saw just ahead and probed continuously for new ideas and new contacts to help them find solutions. Their lack of facade was apparent to teachers, students, and parents. They replaced the pretense that every question had been solved and every problem answered with an admission of how difficult the job was, how far their organization had traveled, and how far they had yet to go. This refreshingly realistic view of their organizations seemed to give subordinates permission to try new ideas, even if they failed after a sincere attempt. Without the false expectation of perfection, orderly experiments could proceed. This safe space for invention meant that bringing in new ideas could become the norm, not a risky aberration.

Related to this openness, the leaders' ability to keep and maintain engaging personal relationships with teachers, students, and staff members enhanced the flow of information they received and increased their chances of encouraging experimenters at just the right time. In the middle of my interview with Northeast Arkansas Superintendent Lee Vent, for example, he asked whether I would like to meet one of the district's strong new teachers. I said that I would, and he telephoned Toni Clayton and invited her to join us. Far from being upset that the central office had called, Ms. Clayton soon joined us and added an important dimension to our talk. Both the superintendent and the teacher were obviously comfortable sharing ideas. The same quality of solid relationships came through at every site. Teachers, almost without exception, raved about their leaders and hastened to explain how central they were to creating meaningful change. The leaders rarely stayed in their offices long, preferring to be out among teachers and students. They cared about their colleagues but were not trapped by an unrealistic desire to keep everyone happy all of the time. Although these leaders had the same responsibilities as their counterparts elsewhere, they did not allow meetings outside of the building or the myriad of pressures that accompany their position to make them remote.

The leaders could also be counted on to keep the school's vision clear and at the center of every decision. Marge Sable spoke eloquently of how improved student learning became the criterion for everything that the Cabot School did. Connie Jones and her successor, Vivian Posey, could be counted on to maintain Three Oaks' commitment to the Core Knowledge curriculum. Montrose Spencer embodied the ideals of the Modern Red Schoolhouse for the

Hansberry School. These leaders did not only agree with the changes in agenda, they had personally identified with those changes.

### ESTABLISHING KEY STRUCTURES

Clearly it is essential to develop a climate that encourages innovative ideas through open dialogue and close professional relationships while keeping the focus centered on mission. However, that is only a first step for effective leaders. They must make these practices operational by establishing supporting structures. At the sites, these structures included shared governance, affiliation with regional or national education groups, a system for sending teachers out to explore, formal communications systems, and quality professional development programs.

### SHARED GOVERNANCE

It would be hard to recount the story of curricular and instructional change at Burruss Elementary without describing that school's commitment to shared governance; the two are just that intertwined. The SUCCESS program in reading and writing described earlier, was the first step Burruss took along the path to curriculum leadership. The way that decision was reached led directly to the evolution of shared governance, a process that has been well documented by two faculty members, Kris Weeks and Julie King.

The origins of the decision to use the SUCCESS program go back to the 1988–89 school year, when some of the faculty, after investigating alternatives to a purely basal approach to language arts, started to use the new program. Teachers gathered information and reported back, and during discussions the principal made it clear that questioning and debates were acceptable and safe. Next, the principal trusted the faculty and showed his respect for their judgment by allowing each member to decide whether or not to switch to the new language arts program.

In the words of Weeks and King, "Making decisions together was a positive experience, and teachers wanted to continue." Encouraged by the language arts experience and supported by the Marietta School Board's requirement that all local schools develop a school improvement plan, the school took on that larger task. Burruss sent a team to the University of Georgia to meet with Carl Glickman and colleagues in January 1990. At the time, Glickman was initiating the League of Professional Schools, with shared governance as one of its guiding principles. The Burruss faculty voted to join the league, thereby linking the school to an important support network.

The school's system of shared governance then went through its own evolution and fine tuning. At first a group of six individuals, called the Leadership Team, assumed responsibility for gathering ideas from the faculty on the school's improvement plan. They soon started to encourage more people to attend the meetings by opening them to anyone with time and interest. These open meetings (called "Ya'll Come" by the staff and principal) led to discussion on broad topics, including the personnel needs of the school. More teachers felt involved in the decision-making process, and the principal also began publicizing the results of the meetings by posting minutes on a bulletin board. The system of representation was also broadened, with a chairperson representing each grade level. The Leadership Team built in a system to bring on new people, which provided a continuing source of new ideas, and the grade levels started to meet on a regular basis.

Leadership Team members attended regular training sessions sponsored by the League of Professional Schools. They also met as a group and became accustomed to the idea of working together to help guide their school—an experience that was beyond what many of them had ever done before. There was a need, however, for more faculty involvement. After reflection and with the advice of consultants from the League of Professional Schools, the Leadership Team made several adjustments to help close the gap between their group and the rest of the school. The Leadership Team renamed itself Faculty Representatives. Teachers who were not representatives were nevertheless sent to league meetings, and, as before, all teachers were encouraged to attend. The staff formed Communication Groups that cut across grade levels, each to be facilitated in its deliberations by a member of the Faculty Representatives group.

The cross-grade structure of the Communication Groups meant that teachers who rarely had the chance to speak with one another about curricular matters were now meeting monthly. The meetings led to discoveries of various kinds, such as unintentional repetition of units, and the staff took corrective steps. Teachers in these groups posed and answered questions dealing with matters such as which skills should be emphasized more to help children move from grade to grade. Just as important, teachers began to invent new ideas for instruction. A sense of cooperation and a search for continual improvement replaced the old image of isolated teachers working in separate compartments of an egg crate. The final question asked in Communication Group meetings became "What can we do to improve instruction at A.L. Burruss?"

Early concerns in the Communication Groups sometimes centered on the mechanics of the school, such as cleaning up the lost-and-found station. Once the groups resolved these issues, however, questions dealing with instruction surfaced. The school started a process of establishing broad annual learning goals, each originating in the Communication Groups. Goals included a move toward thematic teaching; an emphasis on cooperative learning; and improvement of math, science, and social studies instruction. By posting the goals publicly and by speaking about progress continually, the school showed that shared governance was the driving force in identifying and pursuing improved education for students at Burruss.

Shared governance has not stopped with setting and working toward common goals, however. The Faculty Representative group is now called the School Improvement Team. Communication Groups have broadened their membership to include instructional aides, secretaries, food personnel, and custodians. This broader representation brings in many more perspectives and increases the sense of ownership for a wider segment of the community. Finally, a task force system now allows small groups to consider a specific topic efficiently.

Principal Jerry Locke's commitment to shared governance and the time needed to make it work is best summed up in his own words: "Most everything we've done has been an evolutionary sort of thing. We've tried something and if it worked, we kept it. If it didn't, maybe it's taken a long time to change, but eventually it's evolved into something else we'd do."

Burruss is not the only example of a school that takes shared governance very seriously. At Oceana High School, the Academic

Council includes faculty, students, union representatives, administrators, classified staff, and parents. Faculty members vote for their representatives each year, with candidates submitting position papers. Council meetings are open to all members of the school. Principal Lois Jones supports the council's work by encouraging members to share ideas and lead the group. The group considers topics such as applications for major grants, diversity concerns, senior graduation exhibitions, and student portfolios. In addition, the council hears reports from seven committees. Almost everyone in the school serves on one of these committees, which focus on topics such as technology, portfolios, senior exhibitions, and service learning. Faculty members are given time each month to participate in committees. While participation at this level of detail is time-consuming, it seems vital for a school's sense of growth as a community.

Nor are these two examples isolated from the rest of the sites. Sinclair School's Community Council brings together the voices of teachers, parents, community members, administrators, and staff members. This group advises in matters ranging from curriculum and program goals to school budgets and the establishment of priorities. Squires Elementary School participates in Kentucky's site-based decision-making system by having a site-based team comprising the administrator, teachers, and parents. Hansberry Elementary School also has a committee system, with faculty in charge of the key aspects of the Modern Red Schoolhouse plan. The Heron Institute runs exclusively in group format.

## Regional or National Affiliations

As described previously, the League of Professional Schools played an important role in Burruss's development of shared governance. The league gave Jerry Locke and his staff vital support and direction when they needed it and put them in contact with other schools working through the same issues, thus decreasing their sense of isolation.

The advantages of this kind of outside expertise and encouragement are clear. Every one of the sites recognizes this and has had a similar kind of affiliation. Oceana's connection with the Coalition of Essential Schools helped the school set its direction, and the link continues as the school maintains its innovative course. The nine principles of the Coalition appear in school handbooks as a sign of the partnership's central role. Hansberry's plan comes from the Modern Red Schoolhouse project developed at the Hudson Institute. School administrators and faculty members go to the institute for regular training. Three Oaks Elementary School was the first school in the United States to use the Core Knowledge curriculum and is an active member of the Core Knowledge Foundation. Squires Elementary belongs to the National Alliance for School Restructuring, as does the Ridgecrest Secondary School in the Northeast Arkansas School District. Ridgecrest also is a member of the New Standards project and the Coalition of Essential Schools. Sinclair, like Burruss, belongs to an alliance sponsored by a university. In Sinclair's case, it is The Learning Consortium organized by the University of Toronto under the leadership of Michael Fullan. The Verona district belongs to the Village Partnership, a Wisconsin organization that promotes shared governance and site-based councils. The Heron group draws support from the Wisconsin Department of Public Instruction. Cabot had belonged to the National Alliance for School Restructuring. After that connection ended, several teachers at the school reported that they missed the support and contacts.

### OUTSIDE EXPLORATIONS

Another way principals created connections for their schools was by sending small groups of teachers out to explore new ideas, an activity that sometimes included international travel. Carolyn Harden, principal of Oak Grove Elementary School in the Northeast Arkansas School District, exemplifies an administrator who actively searches for new ideas with her staff. Principal Harden and her teachers were able to see multi-age classes in Kentucky, attend a brain-based learning conference in Seattle, and witness innovative practices in Vancouver. Training in Effective Schools research with Larry Lazzotte also proved crucial, changing her thinking and pushing her to look for new strategies to meet students' needs and to help them improve their self-esteem. These explorations were interesting in themselves, but the determination of Harden and her staff to turn those visits into thoughtful innovations in their school was remarkable. Oak Grove's multi-age program, cooperative learning approach, and curriculum integration—all highly innovative for the region—are examples of the value of seeking out new possibilities.

Exploration of the sort undertaken by Oak Grove and other sites is enhanced by the fact that it is strategic. First a possibility is discovered, such as the new approach to literacy at Burruss. Then travel to important schools or conferences is arranged. For Burruss, this included a trip to England to get firsthand information—an honor that made those involved feel great pride in themselves as professional educators.

The schools also took pride in the demand for their expertise from other places around the country. Teachers at Sinclair and their colleagues from other Durham Board schools have become so well known for their advanced skills in cooperative learning that they train faculties around the world. Teachers from Three Oaks Elementary School make presentations on the Core Knowledge curriculum at national conferences and also train school faculties on ways to implement the program. Each time this training takes place, their site makes a new connection, expanding the school's network and helping enrich the lives of the faculty. Jeannie Storm, a 1st grade teacher at Three Oaks, worked with the Hudson Institute when they developed the Modern Red Schoolhouse program and had early contact with teachers at Hansberry as they moved to adopt that program.

## FORMAL COMMUNICATIONS STRUCTURES

Formal methods of communication played an important role in curriculum leadership at these sites. Several of the sites used survey information extensively. Once the schools had dedicated themselves to finding new approaches to curriculum, instruction, and assessment, they could use the objective data derived from these surveys to inform discussions with faculty, parents, and community, moving the conversation from vague impressions to clearer evidence. A spring 1995 community survey of parents, students, and staff at Sinclair Secondary School gave Principal Kaye Egan and her staff important information to use in decision making and in public meetings. They found, for instance, solid support for the Wednesday directed study program and a desire for more choices within the program. If asked about homework loads, the staff could reply that 76 percent of those surveyed (over one-third of whom were parents) said that homework was adequate.

Oceana's use of the community status report sponsored by the American Institutes for Research gave the administrators, faculty, and students vital baseline data in areas such as shared vision, trust, team-work, school leadership, and relations with students at a time when the school needed to absorb hundreds of new students and many new staff members. Starting in 1995, the school joined seven other area high schools, the Bay Area Region Coalition of Essential Schools, John Gardner and the American Institutes for Research, and the William and Flora Hewlett Foundation in a project that resulted in a Community Assessment Guide. All staff and students had an opportunity to respond to the assessment questions. With responses from 68 percent of the staff and 77 percent of the students, the report gave Oceana vital information on the state of the school community in areas such as shared values, trust, and communication. Data from the report helped the staff plan its fall program. Over time, it should provide Oceana with important information on trends in the area of community building and help the school continue to respond to the issue of rapid growth.

Verona's Superintendent Bob Gilpatrick used information from the Village Partnership's climate study to measure changes in atti-tudes in the school board, management team, leadership team, instructional support staff, students, parents, and community. Trends found in the survey helped leaders such as Gilpatrick and Director of Instruction Linda Christensen measure the health of the district and possible areas of future concern.

## PROFESSIONAL DEVELOPMENT SYSTEMS

Many school systems have well-planned professional develop-ment programs. The schools and districts in this study were no exception; in fact, they took professional development one step fur-ther than most, changing professional learning from an important occasional event into a continuing process directly connected to spe-cific stages of the school's development in curriculum leadership. Training of this sort is focused and efficient; its strategic timing and intensity depend upon an open communications system, representing a culture of change, growth, and learning for everyone in the organization.

Sinclair Secondary illustrates this concept well. Professional development at Sinclair does not exist in isolation. Thanks to the work of Norm Green, director of professional development, support for continuing development extends throughout the jurisdiction of the Durham Board. At the Dr. F.J. Donevan Collegiate Institute, where Kaye Egan and several of her key staff members worked before Sinclair was built, Principal Brian Greenway and his faculty use their lunch period to share staff development ideas and train one another in new techniques. Their program, called Toward Learning Cooperatively (TLC), combines team spirit and home-baked desserts, with serious attention to improvements in instruction. On the day of my visit to Donevan, most of the staff had voluntarily come to the TLC session. Once there, we learned how to use multiple-intelligence theory to create a replica of the human digestive system out of such items as pasta and assorted gadgets from home. We then learned how to identify the provinces of Canada from west to east through mnemonics and rap music. The mood was good-natured but focused, modeling the atmosphere the staff wanted to create for students.

Kathy Green, a member of Sinclair's English department, was a strong supporter of staff development at the Durham Board. She traced the progress of the teachers in the Durham Board district to a decision to join the University of Toronto's Learning Consortium. An early goal of that relationship was to set teachers on a course of continuous skill development. In 1988, at their first cooperative learning institute, volunteer teams of teachers and administrators spent several days learning basic techniques and enacting simulations. A culture of developing a deeper understanding of cooperative learning started to spread throughout the district. Now the district offers three levels of training, and Durham Board teachers travel to the United States and Europe to train teachers and administrators. As the curriculum developed, training moved from generic techniques to specific cooperative learning approaches in subject areas such as mathematics and language arts. Teachers use the abundant technology available at Sinclair to produce materials for their staff development activities.

Clearly, it has taken Sinclair and the Durham Board a long time to reach this level of quality. They have had to manage with reduced funding for professional development as well as resist the temptation to lose focus by spreading their efforts too thinly on too many good new ideas. Their culture of encouraging teacher development has been a strong force in maintaining the curricular development for which Sinclair is known.

But staff development at the Durham Board is by no means unique. Oceana brought in experts in Socratic questioning techniques to help teachers improve their skills in this area over the course of several days. Teachers enjoyed having such a resource available during the school day, but they didn't treat this as a unique opportunity. It was an idea that they helped implement and a skill they needed to help Oceana to improve. Summer training for teachers in the Heron group represents a good deal of that organization's efforts. Funding from grants helps to sustain the programs, but teachers' determination to increase their skills to further the kind of learning they believe in is central. In Heron's case this is even more remarkable because the group operates with no school structure or administrative support system in place.

### SUSTAINING POSITIVE RELATIONSHIPS IN THE SYSTEM AND BEYOND THE SITE

Neither the curriculum developments nor the supporting structures at these sites evolved in isolation. All of the work at these sites took place inside complex school systems. In most of the cases, it was the site administrator who took on the job of working with the larger system. In the two districts, the superintendents and their teams worked to create coherence inside of their systems and support for continuing work with their board and community.

Administrators at all of the sites had to oversee the coordination of local curriculum work with district and state plans. For example, Montrose Spencer was responsible for assuring district officials that the Hudson Units being created at the Hansberry School complied with New York City and New York State requirements. Burruss's curriculum and instructional work had to meet the goals of the Georgia Quality Core Curriculum, just as Oceana's changes had to meet the California state frameworks. Sinclair met the goals of the Durham

Board and the province of Ontario when it designed its 9th grade integrated program, and Cabot made sure its standards were consistent with the Vermont Common Core of Learning. No one at any of the sites described the need to comply with district, state, or provincial requirements as a debilitating obstacle. Most of the administrators and teachers simply considered these to be important design requirements.

The administrators faced two important challenges in their dealings with the larger system. First, they had to develop ways for their innovations to be understood without causing jealousy and suspicion. Second, those who created innovative curriculum projects at the lower elementary grades needed to consider the transition of their students to upper grades and deal with the perennial problem of assuring that their students were prepared.

Marge Sable was sensitive to the need to anticipate the possibility of jealousy and suspicion. She brought Cabot's school board members into the school's redesign project early in the process so that they did not feel their policymaking role was being ignored. Heron teachers work with non-Heron teachers and administrators in a continuous dialogue so that the Heron group will be understood and at least tolerated in their buildings. Lee Vent and his team work to spread the good ideas that individual schools in the Northeast Arkansas District have created, thereby moving beyond the tendency to guard site-based projects as "our program."

Ironically, the process of being understood is sometimes more difficult because of the attention these schools receive. One school administrator found that other principals were less interested in the school's curriculum ideas after the school was featured in a magazine article. Another school was held up as "a lighthouse" by one well-meaning superintendent, only to cause the school's principal to fear he was making his colleagues look bad by comparison. In both cases, the site administrators held a lower profile when meeting with peers. This makes perfect sense in terms of interpersonal dynamics, but it may have harmed the system by keeping important information from reaching all schools.

Finally, the fact that some of these schools were new meant that some jealousy inside the system was almost unavoidable. Where new classrooms filled with computers and other technology abound, comparisons ending in hurt feelings seem likely. Here, district administrators helped by making the new site a standard that they wanted every school to reach.

The second tension that the administrators faced was that of transition. "Did I prepare my students for the next level?" is, perhaps, a teacher's most haunting question, and it exists at all levels of education, from early childhood programs to college. Thus, early elementary teachers worry about the expectations of 4th and 5th grade teachers, who, in turn, worry about middle schools, who wonder about high schools, who worry about college or the world of work. In this respect, the sites have developed a proactive attitude based on confidence in their work. Jay Jordan and the teachers at Squires Elementary School worked through such concerns when they created an ungraded primary program. They paid close attention to the opinions of upper elementary teachers in building the program, making sure that they were included in discussions.

At the two schools that use the Core Knowledge curriculum, a movement has developed to spread the curriculum up the grade levels. Conversations between Hansberry and the junior high school housed in the same building have begun, and the higher grades have expressed some interest in exploring Core Knowledge. Some of the Three Oaks faculty felt so strongly about their curriculum that they transferred to their district's junior high school to lay the foundation of a Core Knowledge curriculum there. One principal made an interesting prediction when he told me that in the future, students who have been raised in an exciting, engaging atmosphere where they are actively learning important concepts and facts will simply demand that their education continue to be of high quality or they will disengage. These administrators' concern for their students' education beyond their schools showed that they were serious when they spoke about focusing the work of the school on the individual learner. To assure a smooth transition, these administrators were willing to build bridges inside their system and beyond.

### ANTICIPATING TRANSITIONS

Leaders knew that curriculum innovation in any era involves change—and in our time it involves continuous, fast-paced, large-scale change. All of the sites have had to respond to changing populations and growth. The Cabot School in rural Vermont has had to respond to the needs of new residents along with families who have been in the community for generations. Verona's rapid growth has meant an almost continuous process of school construction. Many new families in Hansberry's Bronx neighborhood need to be integrated into the school's culture and be made to feel part of the community. The town of Paragould, home of the Northeast Arkansas School District, has also experienced rapid growth as a result of the relocation of factories to the area. For the schools that made a fresh start, rapid growth was part of the design. Sinclair, located in a bustling Toronto suburb, had to expand its student population by several hundred over its first three years. The same is true of Oceana, whose population takes in the small town of Pacifica and the much larger community of Daly City, just south of San Francisco.

Growth has meant that new community members and their students needed to be made comfortable. We have already seen how well these administrators worked with the public, both formally and informally. They knew that good communication helps new community members find out about the school and its programs. They understood that the pressures making their communities fluid meant that the compact they had created early in the innovation process needed to be continually reviewed and renewed. They saw this as an opportunity to get fresh perspectives, not as a threat. I asked a college professor who was familiar with one of the schools what the principal would do with a new parent who voiced skepticism over the school's direction. The reply was, "She would ask the new parent to join a planning committee." These leaders had enough confidence to bring interested people into the heart of their programs, even if these people appeared to be less than supportive.

Considering all of the impressive personal qualities of these administrators, the question of their inevitable departure looms large. What happens to the school or the district when the visionary leader moves on? In this case, no pattern emerges because almost all of the sites are in the hands of the original leading administrator. Three Oaks, however, is an example of a school whose original leader did leave in a smooth transition process. Dr. Jones's continuing interest in Core Knowledge provided her with an opportunity to join the Core Knowledge Foundation, which she did. Vivian Posey, the school's new principal, became familiar with the school's curriculum gradually, first as an interested administrator in another school in Lee County and then as Three Oaks' vice principal. Principal Posey spoke about Dr. Jones with the utmost respect. For her, carrying on meant leading a very high-achieving, high-energy staff that was accustomed to developing new instructional approaches to Core Knowledge. Because she had worked at Three Oaks and understood the staff, students, and community, the transition was easier, and the school has maintained its momentum.

While the leaders at the 10 sites can certainly be described as extraordinary, every one of them made clear almost immediately that theirs was a team effort. Central to that team, of course, are the teachers who turn plans into meaningful experiences for their students.

## The Lives of Teachers

Curriculum plans and leadership activities undertaken by principals and superintendents are meaningless without teachers. These schools are exciting places to visit, and that excitement starts with the faculty and the energy they bring to their work. It is teachers' dedication to their students and their willingness to go beyond their normal duties that make these examples of curriculum leadership possible (Figure 3.2 presents a synthesis of the qualities and activities that are typical of teachers who are involved in curriculum leadership). But what is it like to be a teacher in one of these places? What kind of person is attracted to schools like these? How do teachers work cooperatively, how do they invent new programs, and how do they feel about participating in school governance? How do they view professional development? What role do they play in curriculum development?

---

**KEY TEACHER QUALITIES AND ACTIVITIES**

---

**High Professional Standards**
- Engage in constant learning
- Hold high personal expectations
- Demonstrate solid content knowledge
- Possess skills in a variety of instructional models
- Look beyond today's achievements
- See the big picture

**Commitment to Long Hours of Cooperative Work with Colleagues**
- Arrive early, stay late
- Find motivation in the potential of new ideas
- Work as part of a well-balanced, results-oriented team

**"Intrapraneurism"**
- Invent new programs that push the curriculum vision forward
- Follow a logical process of piloting and evaluation

**Participation in Shared Governance**
- Take shared governance seriously
- Help the shared governance system to mature
- Use shared governance to develop new curriculum ideas

**Dedication to Professional Development**
- Master relevant new techniques
- Increase content knowledge
- Learn when and how to integrate disciplines

---

TEACHER TRAITS

Conversations with teachers, principals, parents, students, and district administrators brought forth an image of the kind of teacher who does well at a curriculum leadership school. These teachers, whether novices or veterans, were not interested in finding a comfortable place where they could close their door and work in isolation. They felt they had a good deal left to learn and many new areas to explore. Heron teachers spoke about pushing their own understanding of such fields as mathematics so that they are doing more than speaking about the subject—they are thinking and behaving like mathematicians. Teachers at Three Oaks and Hansberry had to expand upon their content knowledge to reach the expectations of the Core Knowledge curriculum. The faculty at Oceana had to reconsider whole disciplines and merge them without losing the integrity of the core fields. The same could be said of Sinclair teachers as they designed and refined the 9th grade program. Cabot teachers took on the responsibility of designing new standards, establishing grade-level expectations, and then rethinking their own teaching to match their school's direction. One 5th grade teacher at Burruss thought about her classroom atmosphere and told me, "We do a lot of learning together." That attitude also describes the values that the teachers in these schools had for themselves. They did more than speak about lifelong learning. They even went past simply modeling the idea. It seemed as though they had a deep need to continue to learn and explore as an expression of who they were as professionals.

The fact that many of them were working in new schools whose purpose was to reinvent education in fundamental ways only stimulated this attitude. John Thompson, head of guidance at Sinclair, spoke of this as "a rare chance to get a fresh start." Connie Jones, founding principal of Three Oaks, said she wanted teachers who had a love for learning, a love of children, were knowledgeable in their content areas, were high achievers and hard workers, and wanted to be part of something new. For teachers to be selected for Oceana, they had to show excitement, care for students, have a repertoire of teaching methods, be flexible, and be willing to work in teams. In the 750 job or hiring interviews conducted at Sinclair Secondary, a similar set of requirements surfaced.

One reaction to this list may be to shrug and say that everyone would love a faculty like this and schools are lucky to have a few such individuals. But what's the likelihood of finding a whole school full of teachers like these? An impressive feature of many of the sites is that this kind of teacher was in the school system all along. Sinclair hired its faculty from within the Durham Board. Oceana teachers were hired from within their district as well. Some sites also benefited from selective hiring of novice teachers. Three Oaks combined new teachers with veterans in a way that energized both. Hansberry's faculty was enriched by people who were new to teaching but who had had successful careers in fields such as accounting.

### Long Hours and Cooperative Work

Teachers with high energy, a list of accomplishments, solid knowledge of their content areas, a large repertoire of strategies, and a continuing pattern of self-motivated professional growth may sound like a vision of perfection; but all of these traits would not be enough without a willingness to spend long hours planning and a desire to work collaboratively with fellow professionals. No one in this group was interested in the star teacher who performed a well-rehearsed script in isolation.

The amount of time teachers spent planning, meeting, and building model units was impressive at every site. One principal worried that her staff was coming in too often for their own good. For a short time the staff had to return their building keys while a new security system was installed. The principal said that at least then she knew that more of the faculty would stay home during the weekends, but she predicted that they would revert to their old habits as soon as their new keys arrived.

Teachers did not seem worn out or upset at the amount of time they devoted to their schools, but many spoke about their profession as having undergone a serious change. They advised that people should not go into education if they simply like the time off. For these educators, so-called free time was used to sharpen skills, meet with colleagues, help govern the school, plan new units, and keep up with professional reading. The expectations were anything but monotonous, yet the volume of work was undeniably high.

These sites have found that the best way to make fundamental curricular changes is to engage the faculty in teamwork. At Three Oaks, for instance, teachers work closely within grade levels to share materials, develop lesson plans, and design possible art projects. The old pattern of teachers developing model units that they keep to themselves has been replaced with an impressive modeling of cooperative learning. Working in teams allows teachers to focus their energies and benefit from one another's ideas. It also allows the school to avoid buying duplicate materials, because items can rotate from class to class. Hansberry teachers' design of numerous Hudson Units also required great amounts of teamwork. Now teachers can access many units online through the school's computer network.

## "INTRAPRENEURING"

In the 1980s businesses started to refer to a concept called "intrapreneuring." It arose from the fact that corporations had become flexible and open enough to benefit much more often from the inventions of their own employees. Such successful ideas as 3M's Post-It notes were held up as examples of intrapreneuring.

The 10 sites show how that concept can apply to education. The Northeast Arkansas School District is filled with intrapreneurial ideas, ranging from new programs in technology to an innovative early childhood center. A team of teachers at Oceana got foundation support for the development of an integrated algebra class. Combining the talents of teachers in math, arts, and science, this course required new approaches to content and assessment. Teachers documented their pilot carefully and, with the help of a colleague, compared their work with work from a control group. Students helped invent rubrics for the course, and teachers consulted frequently with parents to share student work. The project was successful, and the teachers learned just how much time, patience, and willingness to experiment this kind of inventing requires. The open culture of their school and the support and guidance they received from their Academic Council made this curriculum experiment possible in the first place.

## TEACHERS' VIEWS OF SHARED GOVERNANCE

Just as Oceana's Academic Council supported the integrated algebra course, shared governance played a vital role in nurturing curricular changes at other sites. Shared governance at Burruss made a crucial difference to teachers. As one 3rd grade teacher remarked, shared governance "made a really big difference and is one reason we're successful. It's yours and you're going to take pride in it." Another teacher at Burruss reported that she appreciated the evolutionary path shared governance was taking, getting more serious and setting its sights on student learning. Her hope was that the shared governance group would consider instructional issues even more frequently. A third faculty member liked the idea that her school used shared governance to generate and monitor annual school goals. Teachers understood and appreciated that shared governance took time and required continuous refinement.

### CONTINUOUS LEARNING AND DEVELOPMENT

Teachers at these sites saw professional development as an opportunity for important self-expression as well as growth. Teachers wanted to use the Core Knowledge curriculum at Three Oaks but did not have enough content background. For them, professional development led to enough understanding of concepts and bodies of knowledge to change their curriculum. Burruss teachers wanted to change their literacy program but needed to learn how to use a wider variety of texts in their class. They also needed to know how to connect the various elements of language arts into an integrated whole. Sinclair teachers wanted to teach humanities in an interdisciplinary way. They also wanted to connect science, mathematics, and technology. They believed that a sophisticated understanding of cooperative learning would help them accomplish the task while helping students take more responsibility for their learning. Teachers at Squires Elementary studied how to integrate the disciplines as part of the Different Ways of Knowing curriculum plan. And Heron teachers pushed themselves constantly in their content and methods to grow into their ideal of the scholarly teacher.

In all of these cases, training was not merely someone's or some committee's idea of a good way to spend an inservice day; it was a core element in the school's goal of changing the educational program. Whether new to the profession or veterans, these teachers had replaced the image of having all the necessary skills upon arrival with a demand to continually upgrade and revitalize skills and content knowledge.

### TEACHER INPUT IN WRITING THE CURRICULUM

As the portrait of these teachers becomes clearer, so does the difficulty of their task. One teacher, who had participated energetically in curriculum and instructional development, spoke with real feeling about the changing nature of his school. He seemed proud of their accomplishments but ended by observing, "You know, there is never time to relax and see where we are." With all that teachers need to do, to what extent should they also attend to writing curriculum?

Teacher participation in curriculum development is nothing new. Indeed, large-scale teacher construction of curriculum and instructional materials dates back at least to the early 1930s, when Hollis P. Caswell coordinated the volunteer efforts of 15,000 teachers in the Virginia Curriculum Program (Kliebard 1986, p. 223). Yet, as described earlier, curriculum development can be complex and very time-consuming. These schools illustrate a range of levels of involvement by teachers, from writing almost all aspects of curriculum to adjusting an adopted plan.

Teachers at Cabot, Oceana, Sinclair, and the Heron group are the most involved in creating new curriculum. They represent schools and classrooms where a good degree of flexibility exists, at least at certain grade levels. These teachers needed to confront such basic questions as, How do we organize our program? What are our goals? How do we achieve consistency within and between our courses? What essential questions do we need to respond to? Of course, these teachers were not asked to work in a vacuum. In a departmentalized high school, there may be other groups working on the same issues who may be a little further along. Helpful guides may be available at the school or elsewhere. For the science department at Oceana High School, the California framework represented one such beacon. These teachers also had the school's philosophy, mission statement, and outcomes to refer to during their deliberations.

Cabot teachers worked together to create the school's standards by grade level, but they also had to look at their own courses and see how these related to larger schoolwide directions. For senior high social studies teacher David Book, this meant redesigning his work to include much more hands-on learning and more depth, and being very selective in choosing topics. Other areas, such as science, may require the acquisition of foundational content in order for experiments to be effective, according to another teacher. Teachers in the primary unit referred to their work in curriculum development in language arts and math as stressful but also credited the hard work with results that showed better performance in skill development.

Middle grade teachers spoke about the need for the curriculum to connect beyond the two-year blocks in which they work.

Teachers at Burruss represent a kind of middle ground. Because the Georgia Quality Core Curriculum is specific in its attention to subject detail by grade level, much of the traditional curriculum was decided. For Julie King, instructional lead teacher, the Georgia Quality Core Curriculum was "liberating" because it set up some parameters. Quality Core Curriculum topics drove the school's direction, which freed teachers from simply teaching the textbook. As described earlier, the Burruss teachers built upon this foundation to create a new reading program, thematic teaching, and a series of enrichment programs sponsored by the PTA.

It may seem that teachers using the Core Knowledge curriculum have little curriculum writing to do. Teachers at Three Oaks and Hansberry do use the Core Knowledge sequence as it is written by the Core Knowledge Foundation. However, the Core Knowledge Foundation stresses that their program is meant to occupy no more than 50 percent of instructional time. The remainder may be devoted to local and state requirements and enrichment. Thus, teachers at these schools do have curriculum development responsibilities. In addition, teachers at Three Oaks have produced their own document, called the *Three Oaks Elementary School Core Knowledge Sequence.* This booklet lays out the Core Knowledge program by grade for each month of the year. By agreeing on a monthly calendar of content, the faculty can arrange to coordinate materials and lessons. Students in different classes can compare work on similar projects. Families can refer to the booklet as a guide to help them reinforce their children's lessons at home. In addition, the Three Oaks teachers have spent a great deal of time inventing creative ways to bring the Core Curriculum content to their students. Hudson Units created by the teachers at Hansberry represent the same kind of individual school adaptation of an adopted curriculum. Teachers at both schools mentioned the great amount of time such projects required but also spoke of the satisfaction they took in creating their own approach to their topics.

The amount of teacher participation in local curriculum development varies. It relates to the degree of expectations imposed upon

the school from outside authorities, and how comfortable local educators and the public feel with the idea of taking the time to work
out the learning plan in-house. Another factor is whether a school
has adopted a formal curriculum plan from outside. What seems to
remain constant is the desire of faculty members to have an active
role in shaping the learning program for their students.

Clearly, teaching at a school showing curriculum leadership is
complicated, demanding, and very rewarding. Teachers seemed to
come to these places with a need to stretch beyond their current limits. Whether in early, mid, or late career, educators at these schools
were aware of the opportunities available and were willing to put in
extraordinary effort and time to help the enterprise succeed. They
also came to their work in a spirit of cooperation, since they agreed
that only by working in teams could they hope to redesign the learning program for their students. They enjoyed participating in decision
making as their shared governance projects matured. They saw learning as a lifetime activity for themselves as well as for their students.
In fact, these teachers were wonderful models of adults who love
learning. Regarding curriculum development, circumstances among
sites make a generalization difficult, except to point out that teachers
saw educational planning as central to their role and devoted a great
deal of time to that work.

Anyone who studies these sites leaves with the clear impression
of energized, caring professionals. Teachers spoke often of the children in their classes and their families as the obvious target for all of
their hard work. They realized, of course, that even the best school
with the finest curriculum and instructional program will fall short if
it does not have the support of parents and the larger community.

## Parents and Community Support Groups

Administrators, district leaders, and teachers all make these
schools special. But it is the parents and community who really own
the schools. As we will see in Chapter 4, turbulence comes, in part,
when this support erodes. But what do parent and community
groups do to help schools become and remain curriculum leaders?
What is the range of community support available to these schools?
How might that assistance evolve over time?

Formal community support can be broken into three large categories that describe the community's major function:

- Goal setters and managers
- Supporters and problem solvers
- Hands-on instructors

Although schools are complex organizations existing in even more complex educational systems, the three categories can be arranged in approximate order of their appearance in the life cycle of a school. Thus, goal setters and managers normally appear first, supporters and problem solvers usually come next, and hands-on instructors are third. Several of the sites had more than one of these groups functioning at a time. Figure 3.3 lists the major functions of each group, and the following sections describe some of the best examples of each type.

---

FIGURE 3.3.

**THREE TYPES OF COMMUNITY SUPPORT GROUPS**

---

**Type One: Goal Setters and Managers**
- Often start change
- Help maintain direction
- Serve in an official role

**Type Two: Supporters and Problem Solvers**
- Act as powerful allies to curriculum leaders
- Serve in an unofficial role

**Type Three: Hands-on Instructors**
- Design relevant new projects
- Work directly with students

---

## GOAL SETTERS AND MANAGERS

Goal setters and managers take a broad perspective. They may start the process of curriculum leadership in a community, or others may bring them along to keep things moving after the startup. Cabot illustrates the first case. It was the community task force composed of business leaders, community residents, parents, and teachers that received initial permission from the school board to create higher standards for the K–12 system. The two years that they invested paid off when their school had a new set of educational objectives, won a state challenge grant, and started down the road of reinventing itself. Marge Sable, then principal of Cabot, kept in close contact with the group and coordinated efforts with her staff and her board, but the task force deserves credit for initiating a change in the school's culture. With their task completed, members of the group found other ways to support their school.

The Community Council at Sinclair Secondary School illustrates how a group can evolve from goal setting to helping with management tasks. During Sinclair's first year, a Parent School Advisory was created. This group generated the student learning goals discussed in Chapter 2. Then the Community Council was formed. Its 18 members include students, principal, vice principal, parents, community college representatives, community representatives, business professionals, and parents from sending elementary schools. Although the Community Council does not have power over daily operations, it can express opinions and raise issues. It attends to matters such as student behavior, curriculum, program goals, and school budget priorities.

Districtwide Educational Forums in Verona, Wisconsin, are designed to operate in much the same way as Sinclair's Community Council. The board of education organizes a forum each year, with the board president as chair. Members include central office administrators, parents, teachers, representatives of professional unions, and high school students. Although the forum does not have a policy-setting role, it does discuss issues crucial to the district's development.

A third example of goal setters and managers can be seen at Squires Elementary as part of the Kentucky Education Reform Act, which requires school-based decision making (SBDM). According to state law, each school in Kentucky must have a School Council made up of one principal, two parents, and three teachers. Councils may be larger but they must retain that ratio. It is the job of councils to help their school achieve the Learning Outcomes of the Kentucky Education Reform Act. To accomplish this, councils adopt policies in 18 areas, including curriculum and assessment, staff assignment, student assignment, schedules, instructional practices, and budget (Kentucky Association of School Councils 1995, pp. 2–3). Clearly, the councils have a great deal of authority.

According to the Kentucky Association of School Councils publication *Nuts and Bolts,*

> Curriculum and instruction are the most important policy areas and deserve the majority of your time. Along with assessment, this work is what schools are all about and your opportunity to make the biggest difference for children and for your community's future (Weston and Harmon 1995, p. 51).

The expectations for the councils in the area of curriculum and instruction are significant, shaping decisions that directly affect student learning. Jay Jordan, principal of Squires Elementary, reminded me that the councils are not tribunals. They develop the ground rules for their school and its stakeholders.

Goal setters and managers play an important role in keeping the school's vision fresh and ensuring that its values reflect the larger community. They provide the community with a means for consistent involvement and access to the school.

### Supporters and Problem Solvers

Supporters and problems solvers are critical allies for curriculum leaders. Sometimes these groups exist within the school structure. At other times, they come from outside the school. In either case, this category differs from the first because it does do not play a formal role required by law. Groups in this category normally do not appear until after the school is up and running. However, it would be a mistake to equate their informal or volunteer quality with diminished influence. Organizations of this type are often critical to a school's success.

The Three Oaks Elementary School's Community Resource Team is one example of supporters and problem solvers. An April 1996 combined meeting of the Community Resource Team and the school's PTO illustrates how this group of parents and community members helped school leaders solve problems. After various other matters, the agenda turned to class size. This was a critical issue for teachers, administrators, and parents because they felt that large class sizes would adversely affect students' ability to profit from the Core Knowledge curriculum. One parent seemed to capture the feelings of many in the room when she said,

> As a parent group we have pretty much got to pay attention and follow through on this issue. . . . because we have this Core Curriculum in place which has so much promise and is such an opportunity for our kids. . . . If we ignore the structural issues such as class size you can have the best curriculum in the world and it is not going to matter. . . . That is why it is important that, as parents, we follow through and stay in touch with Mrs. Posey in a supportive, nonconfrontational way.

Vivian Posey and the group spent much of the meeting analyzing the problems associated with class size and considered appropriate ways to work within the district system to alleviate the situation.

Parental support groups can bring effective pressure to bear even under the most extreme conditions. As we will see in Chapter 4, Oceana's parents and community members worked closely and effectively to convince school board members to keep their school open.

Sometimes organizations in this category extend their influence beyond the concerns of one school. The best examples of statewide supporters and problem solvers are the Prichard Committee for Academic Excellence and the Partnership for Kentucky School Reform. Since 1980, the Prichard Committee, which includes some of Kentucky's most influential citizens from a wide range of backgrounds, has worked in the area of educational reform. Executive Director Robert Sexton helped the organization become an early supporter of the Kentucky Education Reform Act of 1990. Now the Prichard Committee works throughout the state to help KERA live up to its potential. One way they do this is by helping regions of the state establish Community Committees for Education, which are designed to be nonpartisan citizen action groups that work locally to help schools and communities discuss education reform in a factual, constructive way. Prichard's director of community support, Bev Raimondo, described one project called Parents and Teachers Talking Together, which brings people together in four-hour facilitated conversations to answer such fundamental questions as, What do we want for our students? How can we get there? What should our priorities be?

At one such meeting, parents and teachers were apprehensive. Some thought that the discussion would simply be a waste of time. By the meeting's end, however, parents saw that the teachers really cared. Teachers saw that parents had positive ideas. They went on to create a newsletter that they sent to people around their county. From there, new topics emerged, public forums were initiated, and a platform for citizens to contribute to the life of their schools was created.

Allied with the Prichard Committee is the Partnership for Kentucky School Reform. This group of business executives is supported by the CEOs of such large companies as United Parcel Service, Ashland Oil, and Humana. Like Prichard, the Partnership for Kentucky School Reform works to bring important issues about educational reform to the public's attention. The partnership brings businesspeople into the classroom to see how KERA works in a local setting. It also supports a speakers bureau as well as a KERA bus, which travels around Kentucky with examples of how education reform works. In a program called Teachers to the Power of Two, the partnership helps get substitute teachers into schools so that full-time staff can visit innovative programs elsewhere.

Although their work may not have an official status, organizations in this category are crucial to the success of curriculum leadership in schools. Through networking and behind-the-scenes activities, they have a quiet but profound impact.

### HANDS-ON INSTRUCTORS

The first two groups act as supporters and indispensable friends as the process of curriculum development gets started. They also help to maintain objective discussions and point out ways to work more effectively. Organizations in the third group are more centered on school-based instruction. They see the school as their home and enrichment of the students' and their families' education as their mission. They often do the work of instruction themselves or in conjunction with staff. Hands-on instructors coordinate with school officials to make their efforts an integrated part of the school's curriculum development.

Burruss's PTA is a model organization in this category. Working with Principal Locke, his faculty, and staff, the PTA finds ways to bring new programs such as Math Super Sleuths into the school. They also bring families to Burruss so that everyone will better understand and support the work of the school. The 1995–96 theme of "My School, My Family, and Me: We Need All Three!" included an open house and a family fun night designed to connect parents with their children's classes. By bringing parents into the schools to try out their children's learning in a hands-on way and by bringing new programs into the school for Burruss students, the Burruss PTA shows how far a volunteer organization can go to increase learning experiences.

Parents can become partners in making instructional material as well. At Northeast Arkansas' Oakwood Elementary School, Principal Ann Lawrence and her faculty are dedicated to the development of a true community school. A central part of this concept is a Parent Center where parents help teachers by making educational games, instructional packages, and related materials. Parents also help by previewing audio-video products. Learning at the Parent Center occurs in both directions. The Accelerated Reader Program helps adults build their skills, and school-based GED classes help parents reach important educational goals of their own while they support the growth of their children.

The Phipps West Farms Beacon Program works with Hansberry Elementary School in much the same way. Dennis Carter, the program's assistant director, explained their work and his own role. Having spent five years in the military, including a year in South Korea, Carter saw the challenges in his home community of the South Bronx in a new light. The neighborhood's problems could be fixed, he felt, but people had to make sacrifices. In his words, "Someone has to stay home and take care of the backyard." And so Carter returned to the South Bronx to share his energies and ideas through this community program. The Beacon Program opens Hansberry's doors to the community, benefiting students, their families, and neighborhood residents. Educational programs reflect Hansberry's Core Knowledge curriculum and cover such topics as mysteries, space, and ancient Egypt. Carter and others from the Beacon Program and the neighborhood built an environmental center behind the school. Teams of people cleaned up the part of the Bronx River that flows by the school, and plans are in the works for an amphitheater. In the future, Carter sees the possibility of a walkway from the school to the Bronx Zoo five blocks away. The goal of making the school and the community one is central to Beacon. "When there is a problem," Carter told me, "the teacher should not feel like an outsider."

The kind of organization parents and community form depends on the school's needs and its stage of development. The key issue is that schools need and benefit from this kind of support. As a major center of community investment, these support groups help the schools on their path to become centers of community education and improvement.

Administrators, teachers, parents, and community members work hard to make education especially valuable for students in these schools. It is important to learn how the students themselves feel about attending a school dedicated to curriculum leadership.

## The Student Perspective

With all of these individuals and groups helping to shape the education of young people, what is it like to be a learner in these schools? Patterns emerge from observations, documents, and conversations with students.

First, students at these schools seem to appreciate that they are attending a school that does things differently. Three Oaks Junior Ambassadors told me their school was more fun than other schools. One girl told me that she was learning some subject matter that her older brother in high school was just starting, which made her feel great. Students also appreciated Three Oaks' continuity. One boy said that they had ended the previous year studying the American Revolutionary War and picked up at the same place the next year. At Northeast Arkansas' Ridgecrest Secondary School, a high school student working for RAM TV beamed with pride as she explained how well her school was using the equipment and how hard they worked to produce television shows for local cable access. Difficult and interesting work could also be seen in the hallways of Hansberry Elementary, where students' posters and projects hung alongside corresponding learning standards. Hansberry students smiled as they spoke about their projects in literature, history, and science. One boy had just won a prize for designing wind- and rubber band-powered toys. The message was clear: The curriculum follows a plan and students connect to that plan continuously.

Ridgecrest's RAM TV and Hansberry's online Hudson Units depend upon technology, which is another part of the lives of students at these schools. Sinclair students spoke of the importance of their school's multimedia computers in helping them create and share new kinds of products of their learning. Oceana's librarian used the school's online capabilities to help students use the newest search engines to find information. At Cabot, students have access to desktop and portable computers much of the time. Verona School District made a comprehensive technology design a central part of their planning. Both students and teachers at these sites are aware of the change that technology will bring to curriculum, instruction, and assessment.

Students at these schools often have a voice in governance. At Burruss Elementary School, students have taken the first step in running a student council. Following the lead of the shared governance model used by adults at Burruss, the students devised their own constitution and committee system. The ideas for subgroups such as the cafeteria committee came from the student body. Students meet every two weeks to work on specific goals. When I asked them why they wanted to do all of this work, they said they simply wanted to serve and change their school. They saw the opportunity as both helpful and fun.

But are these schools for everyone? Oceana students I spoke

with were extremely happy to be there but said some people may not like their school as much. One reason might be the lack of varsity sports. These schools have made choices and have a focus. Families may need to consider their goals and the needs of their children and compare them with the school's direction and, where there is a poor match with the school and other options are available, choose an alternative setting.

Another important aspect of designing education to fit diverse needs is the issue of special education and the ongoing efforts of these schools to extend their curriculum advances to all students. Seen from the viewpoint of special needs learners, these schools work very hard to reach out. At Three Oaks and Hansberry, special educators pointed out that students identified as having special needs work on the same curriculum as all other students. In some cases, this means learning in the general education classroom; in other cases, special-needs students have their own self-contained classroom. Teachers are, however, challenged at times to maintain the same pace and create the same kinds of learning experiences for everyone. At Hansberry the Individual Educational Compact, which resembles an IEP, and the teacher-designed Hudson Units seem to simplify the task of individualizing education by allowing for more individual pacing through the curriculum.

Northeast Arkansas' director of special education, Lark Sigsby, spoke of the importance of inclusion as a way to make sure that all students reach high standards. Curriculum adaptations must sometimes be made, but every student deserves to receive the knowledge, skills, and abilities needed for success. This should not result in watering down the curriculum for special needs students or their classmates. It does mean creating supports for students experiencing difficulties. Inclusion practices should move at a moderate pace, "bubbling up" from the elementary grades, according to Sigsby. One of the district's elementary schools is already deeply involved in this process, but even at higher grades, it is now unusual for anyone to be in a separate classroom for an entire day.

In the same district, Ridgecrest's Project Tree is an example of the attention paid to students in the special education program. Designed for seniors, Project Tree places students in internships in area businesses, where they learn how to succeed in their life beyond school. One student working at a large shelving company was helping the company design a computer program to track orders. While his mentors and I looked on, he showed how his ideas worked and saved the company time and money. He had an important job to do, and it appeared that the connection between school and work had been made.

But none of these facets of student life speak to the issue nearly as effectively as the words of one Oceana student at a dinner meeting. While we were discussing the school's design, curriculum plans, assessment practices, and recent events, this young man smiled, looked me straight in the eye, and said, "What makes our school special is that there is not one student who isn't known by at least one faculty member." Students felt that they were not simply numbers and they were not being batch-processed. The effects were apparent in the side conversations between teachers and students and among students, and in the tone of teachers when they discussed students. These schools had worked hard and had made important progress toward creating caring communities.

In Figure 3.4 we can see how strong community involvement, key administrative activities, and highly engaged teachers provide the structure that supports a positive learning environment for students. Clearly, the support structures and the quality of learning at these sites are impressive and inspiring. The energy, focus, and determination these communities show are exemplary. The same may be said for their inventive spirit. Yet these schools and districts operate in a volatile world. What happens when these sites are overtaken by sudden and dramatic pressure? How can schools showing curriculum leadership survive and even benefit when hit by turbulence? Chapter 4 offers some answers from the experiences of these sites.

## Consider for a Moment

Before we turn to dealing with turbulence, you may want to consider these questions on sustaining curriculum development:

- Is your administrator engaged in key activities? Is the climate

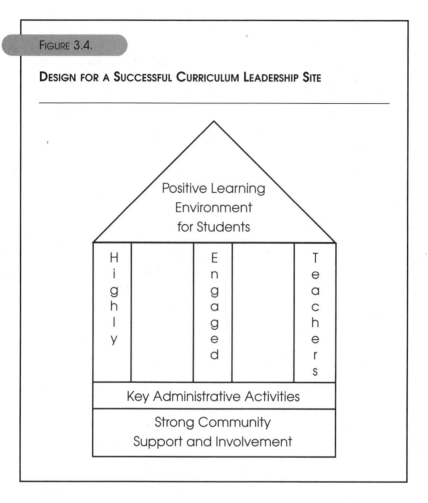

FIGURE 3.4.

**DESIGN FOR A SUCCESSFUL CURRICULUM LEADERSHIP SITE**

Positive Learning
Environment
for Students

High | Engaged | Teachers

Key Administrative Activities

Strong Community
Support and Involvement

for curriculum leadership all that it could be? Are key supporting structures in place? Have transitions been considered? How?

- Does the faculty demonstrate key qualities? Do they share a high standard of professionalism? Are faculty members willing to put in the needed time to move the school? Are shared governance and professional development key values? Is there a willingness to work on curriculum and instructional issues for long periods of time?

- Does the community actively support curriculum development? Does the school have the involvement of goal setters and managers? Supporters and problem solvers? Hands-on instructors?

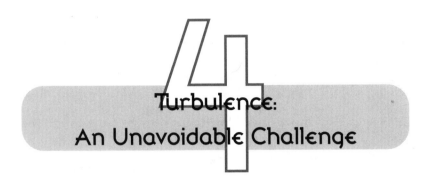

# Turbulence:
# An Unavoidable Challenge

The answer to fear is not to cower and hide;
it is not to surrender feebly without contest.
The answer is to stand and face it boldly,
look at it, analyze it, and, in the end, act.
—ELEANOR ROOSEVELT, *TOMORROW IS NOW*, 1963

Anyone who has flown knows that turbulence is an unstable condition. Gone is the smooth-as-glass feeling of flight. It is replaced with slight bumps, the seat belt sign going on, and a small dread feeling that things might get much rockier soon. But a seasoned pilot sees the same phenomenon very differently. He knows that turbulence can be measured by different levels, that it is often predictable, and that there are specific responses to it. In the case of curriculum leadership, turbulence can also be divided into specific levels that may be encountered at any stage in the development process. Like the experienced pilot, leaders at the sites were able to make needed adjustments and learn from their experience.

Turbulence is a normal part of flying and a normal part of curriculum leadership that can be studied and understood. All of the sites responded successfully to the rough air they encountered. In fact, they often spoke of becoming stronger as a result. What wise planners need to know are the forms turbulence may take, how to respond to it in the short term, and what structural changes might be put into place to enhance stability.

## Three Levels of Turbulence

Manuals on flying categorize turbulence according to specific levels or stages: light, moderate, severe, and extreme. We will consider the first three because the sites provide clear parallels (see Figure 4.1). The fourth level, extreme turbulence, means loss of control and possible structural damage to the aircraft. I did not see any evidence of this at the sites. Perhaps their basic stability brought them under control before the situation degenerated to that extent. What are the qualities of the three levels of turbulence? What examples illustrate those levels? Can one level of turbulence lead to a greater degree of instability if left unattended? The following sections describe the various kinds of turbulence, using examples from the sites, and later sections relate how the sites dealt with these challenges.

### LEVEL ONE: LIGHT TURBULENCE

For many people light turbulence is normal flying. There are slight vibrations and small dips. However, a sensitive observer can see signs of stress. The key is that people continue to work normally because the issues causing the turbulence are ongoing. Causes of light turbulence in schools include (1) the disjointed community, (2) isolation, and (3) issue overload.

#### THE DISJOINTED COMMUNITY

Not one of the sites was completely homogeneous in demographics. Even rural areas had different levels of income and education that became important at times. However, the related issues were more pronounced in three cases and received formal attention.

The Burruss Elementary School in Marietta, Georgia, serves two somewhat distinct communities. One is a largely white, middle-class neighborhood surrounding the campus, and the other is a predominantly minority, less well-off neighborhood in a different part of town. Children from the immediate area may come from families that

FIGURE 4.1.

## THE THREE LEVELS OF TURBULENCE

### Level 1: Light Turbulence
Characteristics:
- Associated with ongoing issues
- Little or no disruption in normal work environment
- Subtle signs of stress

Possible causes:
- Disjointed community
- Isolation
- More good new ideas than the system can handle (issue overload)

### Level 2: Moderate Turbulence
Characteristics:
- Widespread awareness of the issue
- Specific origins

Possible causes:
- Rapid growth of the community and student body
- Communication problems with upper grades
- Loss of an important support

### Level 3: Severe Turbulence
Characteristics:
- Fear for the entire enterprise
- Possibility of large-scale community demonstrations
- A feeling of crisis

Possible causes:
- Community values conflict
- External threat to the school's future—the mega-issue

have had long contact with the school. Families who live across town may not have such long-term ties.

This distinction became clear when teachers and the PTA were planning a family fun night. Students, administrators, teachers, and parents spent many hours designing an evening when families could visit their children's classrooms to see the results of their learning. It was going to be a time when the curriculum could come alive, important questions could be answered, and families could become connected to innovations in such areas as whole language and inter-disciplinary learning. Members of the planning committee were worried, however; how could they get people from all neighborhoods served by the school to attend? In the past, parents who lived nearby found it easy to come and were well represented. Many fewer families came from a distance. This meant that one group of parents would have a rich, hands-on understanding of the school's curriculum direction while the other would remain disconnected.

Three Oaks Elementary School in Fort Myers and Hansberry Elementary in the Bronx faced a nearly identical problem. Three Oaks serves two distinct areas, one close at hand and the other a long bus ride away. Educators and families are concerned about the coherence of the community. Hansberry's students come to the school from several neighborhoods. In addition, nearly half of the students come from homes in which English is a second language. Bringing families of Hispanic origin together with African American families is a major focus.

## ISOLATION

As one might expect, serious, sustained curricular development cannot occur in a vacuum. Teachers and administrators need partners outside of their organization to help them reflect and solve complex problems. One common theme that I heard across all of the sites was how easy it was to feel alone in the effort to change the curriculum and the life of the school.

Teachers in the Heron Institute spoke about being isolated in their buildings because they were often the only member of the Heron group in their grade level or even in their school. Teachers felt misunderstood by peers and administrators. They did not have daily access to other members of the group to discuss instruction and curricular questions.

## ISSUE OVERLOAD

Sometimes an institution must deal with an oversupply of good new ideas. The desire to start great enterprises can be so powerful and the rewards so stimulating that leaders can forget that invention needs to be balanced with discretion. The sites appeared to be able to handle only a finite number of new directions before teachers and even administrators started to complain about having too full a plate. In an overstimulated environment, it is not clear where the focus needs to be and which efforts can wait. A sense of frustration can develop, even among teachers and administrators who want to keep their institution moving.

A sizable cross section of educators in the Northeast Arkansas School District agreed that their agenda was full. In all, the district had taken on more than 60 new initiatives within four years. These ranged from a program that gave high school students hands-on experience in running an aquaculture lab to a ham radio class. All of the initiatives had a direct implication for the curriculum. Superintendent Lee Vent remarked, "It is time to take a long hard look at all of the new programs." With so much power at the sites, the district could end up with a "hodgepodge." They needed to know which initiatives were working well and which needed to be put aside. Until the district faced this source of turbulence, further work on the learning agenda seemed to cause more distraction than anything else.

### LEVEL TWO: MODERATE TURBULENCE

When flying through moderate turbulence, the plates may be rattling, the seat belt sign is probably on, but lunch is still being served. Moderate turbulence in schools gets almost everyone's attention. People face the issue differently, but it is hard to avoid hearing people speak about it. You know that there is moderate turbulence when the topic comes up in almost every encounter either as a current issue or something significant in the recent past. Examples of moderate turbulence include (1) rapid growth of the school community, (2) communications issues with upper grades, (3) tension-filled conditions, and (4) loss of an important support.

### RAPID GROWTH OF THE SCHOOL COMMUNITY

Every site tried to create a personalized learning experience for their students. For many, this was central to their existence. The greatest challenge the sites faced was a rapid increase in the size of their student body. In some cases this problem was part of the innovation itself—the school either became so popular that its population ballooned or it grew because of an agreement with the superintendent.

Planned growth occurred at Oceana High School and Sinclair Secondary School. Both schools were allowed to start small in order to establish their new approaches without the pressure of large numbers of students. Oceana started its new life with fewer than 400 students. By agreement, that number was to grow by about 200 per year. One teacher commented that the small class size at the start was a great advantage in getting to know students. With growth, the school had to respond to many more students as well as the addition of new faculty. Whereas once parents applied to send their children to Oceana, now the district's policy required the school to admit all students who wished to attend. Similar conditions existed at Sinclair, which had to accommodate the dynamic growth of housing around the school.

Ironically, increased popularity also carries a crucial challenge: How can the schools keep the intimate sense of community among students, teachers, and families when large numbers of new people are arriving each year?

### COMMUNICATIONS WITH UPPER GRADES

When an entire district takes on the job of curriculum leadership, teachers in lower grades can feel confident about their students' development. The philosophy and approach that they initiated will continue. However, at many of the sites described in this book, elementary school teachers worried about the disjuncture between their classrooms and those of their colleagues in upper grades. Concern over transition from Kentucky's primary unit to upper elementary grades was an issue at Squires Elementary School, but at least they had a committed principal, community support, and general faculty agreement on curriculum direction. This was not the case for the Heron group, which faced difficulty in part because of the isolation described earlier. There was no "Heron School" with a consistent approach or shared philosophy. How would junior high school teachers who were not part of the group understand the strengths that Heron students brought to class? Who would work with the teachers to clear the air?

## TENSION-FILLED CONDITIONS

The Effective Schools research of the 1980s reported that even in the most difficult neighborhoods, some schools are able to create a secure community for learning. Life might not be comfortable outside of the school, but it could be controlled inside so that learning could take place. At Hansberry the building was well organized, learning was clearly going on, and teachers and administrators knew their students and interacted comfortably. But both minor and serious problems cropped up at a rapid pace. Teachers and administrators seemed to have their hands full meeting the needs of their students. This was not a temporary problem; it was part of life at that school.

## LOSS OF AN IMPORTANT SUPPORT

The Cabot School had been a member of the National Alliance for School Restructuring, but it suspended membership in that organization at the end of the 1993–94 school year. Several teachers at this rural K–12 school said they missed the alliance membership because it was an important contact for them during a period of change. At Verona, the overhaul of education at the state level meant that the Wisconsin Department of Public Instruction, the place that many looked to for leadership in curriculum design, might not be there for support and encouragement. Some at Verona felt that they were now alone.

## LEVEL THREE: SEVERE TURBULENCE

Severe turbulence has everyone's attention. Food service stops, and the pilot's soothing voice may not be enough to calm everyone down. In the air and at schools, severe turbulence may be predictable, but it may also come on suddenly. In schools, people have a sense that the whole enterprise may be at risk. Severe turbulence conjures up images of a high school gymnasium filled with hundreds of angry parents, television cameras, and a school board not up to the job. Two general conditions are associated with severe turbulence: (1) community values conflicts and (2) the mega-issue.

## Community Values Conflicts

Public schools must serve an entire community. This means providing an education for children from families with widely varying values and priorities. At Sinclair Secondary School, the integrated approach to 9th grade studies and the Wednesday program that emphasized student freedom drew heated attention from some parents in the first year. The amount of latitude in these programs seemed ideal for some families but made others uncomfortable. A version of the movement against outcome-based education hit several of the districts, including the Northeast Arkansas School District.

In Verona the currents of community values divided into two groups, one calling itself Return to the Basics and the other Back to the Future. Interviews with members of both groups showed a common level of respect for the importance of schools and passion for the need to help them to succeed. The differences came when people defined what schools needed to emphasize. As at many other sites nationally, issues related to values education, portfolios, alternative report cards, whole language, and authentic assessment entered the discussion. This difference created a deep split in a district that had prided itself on faithful community support, innovation in curriculum, and a statewide reputation for excellence. Because earlier goal setting had involved large public meetings, school administrators believed that they were supported by a great majority of the community. Board elections and even relations between residents on opposite sides of the divide became stormy.

An irony in curriculum leadership is that the very act of changing old assumptions and moving the learning agenda into new areas may seem both an imperative and a risk. Some elements of the communities at almost every site complained that schools should spend more time doing traditional things well and less time inventing new ideas. This feeling became sharper when schools accompanied their curriculum changes with changes in the way they evaluated learning. Changes in traditional report cards and the use of portfolios raised anxiety in parts of the community.

## THE MEGA-ISSUE

Every day schools face external conditions that challenge them. Perhaps their state's economy hits a rough spot and residents vote down a budget proposal, or a new law requires the teaching of drug and alcohol prevention to all 7th graders. These are simply part of the normal life of schools and districts. Mega-issues are different. Whereas normal external events are like small meteors that cause short bursts of bright light while they burn up in the atmosphere, mega-issues are like a comet headed straight for the school. The atmosphere (or the normal administrative process) is not going to handle a problem of this size. What makes this situation particularly difficult is the fact that, like the comet, the mega-issue seems to come from out of the blue. This form of turbulence is a real and most unwelcome surprise.

Supporters of the Kentucky Education Reform Act at Squires Elementary School and elsewhere in Kentucky faced such a mega-issue during the 1995 race for the governorship, when the reform effort itself became a hot campaign topic. Detractors of the ungraded primary program and the assessment program used this political race as an opportunity to try to reverse a trend that they did not like. It appeared that the whole educational reform program, including the items related to curriculum leadership, might be dropped. On a smaller but no less dramatic scale, Oceana High School faced a decision by district administration to close its doors, not because of disagreement on the school's direction, but simply as part of a larger reorganization plan. As in Kentucky, the whole enterprise suddenly seemed in jeopardy. How can reform continue under these circumstances?

## Taking Action

A sensitive leader—whether an airline pilot or a principal—needs to pay attention to turbulence at any level. At the least this means monitoring light turbulence and keeping everyone aware of conditions. More typically, it means taking action. Of course, schools, like airplanes, can fly through lots of bumpy air for a while. Sometimes, there is no other choice. But many circumstances worsen with inaction. Opportunities for early smaller corrections are fleeting, and today's problem of the disjointed community may turn into tomorrow's revolt of alienated factions and next week's catastrophic school board elections. Knowing that action is required in the face of turbulence is important but not sufficient. How did these schools and districts work through their patches of bumpy air? What should be done when light, moderate, or severe turbulence strikes? Let's look at the strategies these schools used to reestablish stability.

### DEALING WITH LIGHT TURBULENCE

The Northeast Arkansas School District's problem of issue overload offers good insight into how light turbulence can be handled. The first sign that the overload problem was being dealt with was the openness with which people talked about it. Everyone from the superintendent to teachers, board members, administrators, and parents admitted the district had too many initiatives going on at once. Neither defensiveness nor blame stood in the way of action. People simply spoke about the problem as part of where their course had taken them. This was normal and they had a strategy to deal with it. Instead of complaining, most people found that they were in the part of the cycle of growth that required reflection, analysis, and strategic decisions. The system's culture had been transformed so that people understood and accepted this.

Recognition of a stage of the growth cycle is a good first step because it shows a reasoned and objective approach to an issue. But the situation requires a specific response. In this case, this meant hiring an outside consultant to conduct a process called Future Search. At one of the Future Search sessions, groups of administrators, parents, students, teachers, businesspeople, central office staff, and board members gathered in a large gymnasium to work on their problem. Participants wrote down lists of which district achievements they were most proud of and areas where they felt the district could have done better. Principals, for instance, were proud of the many staff development and travel opportunities given to teachers but were concerned about dysfunctional families, attendance problems, and some initiatives that had not worked. Parents praised the many different school programs, such as the high school's cable television channel, but they worried about a lack of involvement between

122

some parents and their children; they also spoke about drug use and discipline problems. The business group gave high marks to the partnership program between the schools and area businesses, the district newsletter, and the school-to-work program for special education senior high school students.

Dr. Faye Cox, who guided the Future Search process, described the group's work. Early on, these stakeholders looked at the past three decades and considered what had affected them as individuals, what was going on in the world, and what was going on in the district. Interestingly, students learned some important historical lessons about their community as described by older members of the large group. They and the other groups gained meaningful historic perspective on the conditions that shaped their lives and the agenda for their schools. A follow-up step was the creation of a mind map, in which all stakeholder groups added their ideas to a large chart depicting personal, world, and district events. In this way, everyone could understand large trends and how they related to their own stakeholder group.

Plans for further meetings centered on what each group saw as an ideal condition for their district in the coming decade. What were the possibilities? What roadblocks did each small group see from its perspective? Where could people from the different sides agree and where would they have to agree to disagree? This discussion would result in action plans for district leaders and the board.

Dr. Cox found the group to be open and willing to tackle new tasks. Businesspeople in the room were especially comfortable with this problem-solving model because they were familiar with its uses in industry. Others also were enthusiastic. Future Search appeared to be an important process. First, people appreciated having a professional consultant guiding the group through complex issues. Second, this approach gave community members a pathway into the often abstract world of school reform. Groups could see how their stories fit into the larger pattern of community and school district development. Understanding larger patterns and cycles of change may have given the residents of this community some power to respond early to new conditions such as rapid industrial growth and changing demographics that appeared to loom large on the horizon. A program such as Future Search is a reasonable response to the problem of light turbulence because it emphasizes involvement, multiple perspectives, and flexible future planning. Because the schools still enjoyed a high level of trust, participants could focus on building a positive future rather than correcting something broken in the present.

The movement to proactive behavior typifies responses to light turbulence. Burruss Elementary School responded to its light turbulence issue of the disjointed community by organizing bus rides to and from important evening events for families in the most distant part of the community. This was not seen as a panacea but simply one way to start to make contact with a key group of families who might not have had transportation. This also pushed planners from simple awareness of a problem to some initial action.

Hansberry responded to its problem of the disjointed community through a highly organized program of bilingual education in which the goal called for every student to become bilingual and biliterate in a multicultural setting. Bilingual Coordinator Maria Matos said, "The future of tomorrow is knowing more than one language." Therefore this school of 475 students offers two dual language classes where Spanish is taught to English-only speakers and English is taught to Spanish-only speakers, as well as five bilingual classes. Students whose first language is Spanish are taught to understand English and the reverse is also true.

The light turbulence caused by isolation resulted in different responses by the Heron group. For the Heron teachers, their very design meant that they would likely not have colleagues in every corridor of every school. Understanding that they probably would work alone, the organizers of the group structured evening meetings to discuss events and share strategies. This seemed to be enough to keep the group together. Clearly, the summer training opportunities were also important supports.

Schools and districts seemed to deal well with light turbulence when they recognized these disturbances as a normal part of their existence and built in solutions that were equally predictable. The Future Search process came at a predictable time, when the district had too many good ideas and its coherent direction seemed to be threatened. Burruss's bus for distant community members, the Heron group's evening meetings, and the bilingual program at Hansberry were all strategies intended to meet recognized problems that were part of the fabric of school life. Responding to these kinds of problems is important and well within the range of typical group activity. But how do schools and districts respond to the more novel and overwhelming waves of rough air encountered in moderate turbulence?

### Dealing with Moderate Turbulence

When Oceana faced a large influx of new students and new faculty members, teachers and administrators decided to handle the problem with intense, focused planning. The question was not simply one of orienting hundreds of new people in the ways of Oceana's system; it also meant redefining Oceana's culture to reflect new members. A job of this size required detailed planning, objective information, and time.

The school decided to make community building the focus for its August inservice days, which became a kind of retreat. Participants worked for three days to define what the Oceana community was and to plan specific ways to help it deal with rapid growth as comfortably as possible. The group considered data about Oceana and found that they had a solid school community in place. They also asked themselves how community building related to the school's restructuring plans, as well as how they could enhance the feeling of community. By doing this, the group was finding ways to see consistency between the challenge of expansion and their larger plans for restructuring. This placed the moderate turbulence into an understandable pattern that could be planned for and dealt with. The retreat itself showed recognition that this was a high-priority issue.

Flowing from the retreat were plans for a special orientation for freshmen and other students. At the orientation new students would get to meet current Oceana students. The school's student advisory program also gave students a chance to discuss in an organized way their feelings about coming to a new school. Many of the new students came from a high school that had been closed as part of a district plan. Special sensitivity for the feelings of these students as well as their families also became a priority. Printed material, such as the school handbook, helped familiarize new students, parents, and teachers with Oceana, and so distribution became a priority. The handbook included pragmatic information such as a map of the school, Graduation Standards, and admission information for California's state university system. It also highlighted Oceana's philosophy, Outcome Statements, and assessment and portfolio program, as well as key projects such as community service and Senior Exhibition. In addition, every classroom displayed the school's Outcomes and Common Principles.

Conversations with administrators, teachers, students, families, and staff members revealed an equally powerful informal process taking place. These people had internalized the significance of the issue of rapid growth, saw it as everyone's responsibility, and adjusted their behavior to meet the challenge. New members would not be isolated. Everyone needed to take time to know them, understand how they might be feeling in a strange setting, and help them through a tough transition. The principal, vice principal, and guidance director were even more visible than usual during the early weeks of the fall semester to make sure that things flowed smoothly. No one expected perfection, and even though families had selected Oceana, not every new student or faculty member made the transition perfectly. Still, four months into the school year, the new group seemed to be well integrated. The feared division did not materialize, quite possibly because the school had designed a strong and focused response and the school community as a whole took ownership of that response.

Teachers in the Heron group shared the outlines of a planned response to their issue of moderate turbulence—how to provide for a smooth transition for their students into non-Heron classrooms. One Heron teacher found that a recent graduate of his class, who had been very successful in math, had been placed in a low-ability math group by her next teacher. Realizing the problem, the two teachers met for an in-depth conversation. At the meeting, the Heron teacher showed the student's previous work to demonstrate her strengths in mathematics. The meeting took more than two hours but resulted in the student's being placed in the highest-level group. Now this Heron teacher meets regularly with middle grade teachers, parents, and students.

Like the community-building retreat at Oceana, the first step of problem recognition was quickly followed by steps toward making a predictable response that fit the values of the curriculum leader. Individual attention and building upon the strengths of learners were important elements in the Heron group's teaching. Thus, individual attention and pointing out the strengths of students became part of the response. The next step was to make the response part of the system. For Oceana this means regularly checking the quality of school community life with the help of the American Institutes for Research survey project. For Heron members this means planning regular meetings with teachers receiving their students. In both cases, leaders take responsibility for the issue and devise responses.

### DEALING WITH SEVERE TURBULENCE

Verona shows how a district can deal with severe turbulence and come out feeling stronger. It also shows a possible relationship between levels of turbulence. In Verona's case, rapid growth has been a dynamic force, as the district's reputation for good schools and its location close to Madison brought growth at the rate of more than 200 students a year for seven years. This meant new families, a succession of bond votes for new schools, and an implied demand for heightened communications. At the same time, district administrators, teachers, board members, and representatives from the community met in a strategic planning process.

One highly visible product of these meetings was a statement of what were called Essential Learner Outcomes, which described qualities that each district graduate should have. These included being a person who accepts challenges of living, a learner who creates knowledge, a family member who collaborates with others, a contributor who values culture and diversity, a steward who promotes and protects people and the environment, a citizen who acts with civic consciousness, and a producer who uses skills to attain significant goals. While some considered these statements to be a reasonable list for students facing the new century, others in the community saw the learner outcomes as part of a larger movement toward outcome-based education. Despite strong statements to the contrary by district leaders, some members of the community started to identify Verona's direction with a larger national movement they felt uncomfortable with. One member of this group reported that his complaint about OBE was that there was little proof that these ideas really worked. He feared what he saw as a move away from such traditional approaches as phonics, standardized tests, and report cards. Other issues such as the perceived value judgments in the Essential Learner Outcomes sparked debate.

From this point, board elections, which were normally tranquil affairs, heated up, becoming contests between supporters of the district's Learner Outcomes and those favoring what they called basics. Professional relations and even friendships came under great stress as the community voted for its new board leaders. Not surprisingly, the board was split, with three members on either side of the divide, one person in the middle, and a new chair who decided to dedicate herself to finding common ground.

Then Verona's story took an important turn, bringing four positive forces into play. First, the superintendent and central office leaders decided to shift the focus of decisions from hot political issues to less emotional areas where consensus could be reached. Superintendent Bob Gilpatrick got the board to focus on passing a referendum on a school construction project and a district technology plan. By paying close attention to the concerns of individual board members and by working for consensus as often as possible, these initiatives passed the board level and received wide support in the community. Thus everyone saw that the district may have been divided on some issues but it could still respond to important needs.

Second, the community was fortunate to have a skilled and self-sacrificing person agree to become chair of the school board. While she supported some of the changes in Verona, her status as a trusted community member allowed her to work with all sides. Certainly, many of the new ideas that grew out of the Essential Learner Outcomes were worthy. But the district had not communicated thoroughly enough with its citizens. Important ideas, such as not moving too quickly to replace report cards with portfolios, seemed to get lost under the pressure to invent a school system that was up to tomorrow's standards. The board chair saw the split vote in the board election as a community warning. Community members were telling educators to be careful, to stop speaking educationese, and to slow down. One of her early missions was to clear up misunderstandings concerning just what the schools were doing. In the heat of a political campaign, distortions and accusations seemed to fly recklessly. She also listened carefully to all opinions. She made it her business to go into the community and seek out ideas. This included frequent trips to the schools to listen to teachers and students.

These two elements set the stage for the third positive force, the creation of a Strategic Planning Council. Unlike previous efforts, this group—including 4 board members, all principals, the superintendent, the director of instruction, 1 teacher per school, and 12 community members—was selected to represent all sides in the debate. Members met in four-hour sessions throughout the spring and summer of 1994, guided by a skilled and sensitive facilitator from the community who had served on a district board elsewhere in Wisconsin and had professional experience in getting groups to build understanding. The broadcast of these meetings on local-access cable television enhanced their open quality.

Deciding on an agenda for these meetings was crucial. The group decided to attempt to rewrite the district's mission and Essential Learner Outcomes—an indication that the turbulence in Verona went right to the heart of things. Interesting changes in group behavior occurred over the course of the meetings. At the first meeting participants tended to focus on position statements, whereas at the last meeting, people from different sides were working to build ideas together. The end result of the process was a new mission statement, called Educational Goals, which includes statements of academic achievement and what are now called "character goals." The group also made its position clear on such issues as the learning environment, student assessment, system assessment, and follow-up initiatives to implement the district's goals. Although complete consensus proved to be elusive, almost everyone in the group could unite around the new statements. In a way, they seemed to believe that the Strategic Planning Council was the district's last best chance to bring people together.

The fourth force, and the one upon which the others seemed to depend, was the underlying strength and stability of the district.

Severe turbulence was not the norm in Verona, which enjoys a reservoir of good will and strong community affiliation. Many new people have moved to the area, but many more have spent decades in Verona. In addition, the schools had received important outside recognition for high performance at relatively low cost from such outside sources as the Wisconsin Manufacturers and Commerce Association. In fact, standardized test scores remained stable through the period of turbulence. This lends credibility to Director of Instruction Linda Christensen's observation, "You cannot sustain unhappiness very long."

Verona was a changed place in 1995. While no one supposed that the district was immune from future turbulence, perhaps just as rough as before, most people said that they were stronger as a group for having gone through very difficult times. Bob Gilpatrick explained that Verona was changing from a school system to a system of schools. The principle of being a system of schools can perhaps best be seen in the district's new charter school movement. Verona has become the leader in Wisconsin for starting such schools. The schools follow different curricular directions—for example, one features teachers working closely with parents and students to plan individualized learning experiences, and another features Hirsch's Core Knowledge curriculum and a direct instruction model—but they share a common emphasis on flexibility and choice within the public school setting. The role of the district has been to help assure that whatever the particular emphasis of a charter school, students all achieve agreed upon standards of performance.

Oceana's encounter with severe turbulence meant dealing with the possible closing of the school. Although the threat had nothing to do with Oceana's performance, the very possibility could have dispirited faculty, students, and families. That never happened. Instead, key elements of the community went to work. Principal Lois Jones spoke about her role in maintaining a good education for students throughout the crisis by upholding the core principles of her school: "Part of our culture is caring; it is one of the building blocks of our school." If the focus of Oceana was the creation of a caring community where students became responsible for their own learning, the possibility of closing the school was a test of that arrangement.

School leaders began to speak to parent and community groups. Because Oceana had worked closely with parents to start its new program, it received a strong positive response. Parents and students worked as a team to invite school board members to see what they were doing in the school. Teachers and parents also reached city officials in their effort to save the school. Community members without children in the school also helped—an outgrowth of the required community service program. Students and their school were known in the area; people appreciated the students' involvement and supported Oceana when severe turbulence hit.

School board members were impressed by the outpouring of support and equally impressed by the calm and methodical way that support was marshaled. School leaders received and appreciated help from such outside organizations as the Coalition of Essential Schools. Certainly that kind of testimonial added credibility to their case. But the determining factor in saving the school seems to have been the small army of parents, students, and teachers who convinced school board members and district officials that Oceana deserved to stay open. For Oceana, having an open system in which every group knew about the school and participated in its decisions helped the school survive a threat to its very existence.

The governor's race in Kentucky was something far beyond the control of the school community at Squires Elementary. Yet, because the entire state education reform program became a campaign issue, the election outcome could have had an immense impact. Grassroots school-based decision-making programs had brought community members into schools with real power. Organizations such as the Prichard Committee, with its long-standing reputation for high-quality work, and the Kentucky Partnership had brought information about the state's reform efforts to large numbers of people. The candidate supporting the Kentucky Education Reform Act won by about 20,000 votes, and the reform effort was saved. In this case, support for KERA from many directions was more powerful than criticism. No one with whom I spoke, however, thought that the election ended the discussion of KERA's future. The possibility of future severe turbulence seemed to underscore the importance of engagement and cooperation with many elements of the wider community.

In Verona, Oceana, and Kentucky, severe turbulence came from forces beyond the school buildings and, likewise, was resolved with the help of people beyond the schools. These sites employed the opposite of a bunker mentality. Parents and community members were brought into the very core of the process, and their ideas proved crucial. School administrators helped their sites focus on learning by emphasizing calm during crisis. In Verona's case, this meant turning the board's attention to matters on which they could agree. In Oceana's case, the goal was running the school as close to normal as possible, even when times seemed their worst. But the experience of going through turbulence also created some lasting changes at the sites.

## Lessons Learned from Turbulence

Figure 4.2 presents strategies educators can use to deal with the three levels of turbulence. As indicated by the various examples presented in this chapter, schools and districts succeeded when they treated turbulence as a normal, if difficult, part of curriculum leadership. They all viewed their situation in strategic, rather than personal, terms. Leaders, especially, took on the responsibility of analyzing circumstances carefully and responding with measured action. They were quick to bring in help when they needed it and did not try to facilitate by themselves. This set of behaviors became a model for others in the organization to follow. The focus changed from fear to positive response. Confidence in the basic soundness of the school, its professionals, and their community helped these schools navigate through the roughest storms.

## Consider for a Moment

As you can see, turbulence may take varied forms and may come at almost any time. If you think turbulence is on its way to your school or district, here are some questions that may help you respond:

- What level of turbulence are your dealing with—light, moderate or severe?
- Have you planned an appropriate, immediate strategy?
- Have you prepared yourself and your organization to respond as objectively and as openly as possible?
- Are you operating with clear data or with opinions?

---

FIGURE 4.2.

### STRATEGIES FOR DEALING WITH THE THREE LEVELS OF TURBULENCE

**Level 1: Light Turbulence**
- Build in predictable reactions to these normal bumps.
- Establish regular meetings and problem-solving teams.
- Be highly inclusive; establish support systems.
- Keep working on the issue in the most open way possible.
- Measure progress and report results.

**Level 2: Moderate Turbulence**
- Define the scope of the problem.
- Raise the issue high on the priority list.
- Dedicate blocks of uninterrupted time to solve the problem.
- Stay open to new possibilities—avoid defensive behavior.
- Create and use a variety of clear communication tools.
- Implement specific solutions following a clear schedule with a feedback loop.

**Level 3: Severe Turbulence**
- Avoid a "bunker" mentality.
- Keep in mind the basic stability of the school.
- Be prepared for the birth of new possibilities and an altered organization.
- Be prepared for personnel changes.
- Emphasize a deep process that involves all segments of the community.
- Keep people as objective as possible.

---

# The Sum of the Parts

Clearly, curriculum leadership is a complicated process that involves a number of important elements. As we have seen, the broadest of these include building a solid foundation on which to organize curriculum leadership, choosing a path to follow, sustaining development over time, and overcoming the inevitable turbulence.

## On Organizing Curriculum Leadership

Schools appear more likely to succeed as curriculum leaders if the fundamentals are in place. Curriculum leadership requires steps that are logical but not always attended to; and when these steps are overlooked, the blame for failure too often falls on the innovators when it really should rest with a poorly prepared system that was not up to the task of supporting serious change in the first place. As Maslow reminds us, safety and security come before creativity. Issues such as safety, attendance, faculty morale, good communication with families, and basic academic success were reasonably secure at these sites before they attempted further steps. If these issues have not been addressed in your setting, it is probably wise to concentrate on them first.

Similarly, it is useful to consider the qualities of the individuals who will lead the effort. Leaders at the 10 sites shared qualities that helped them do their work effectively. They were strong but in new, more subtle and inclusive ways. They grew as their organizations grew and always looked forward.

Starting any process is challenging, often because it is not clear where to begin. In the case of curriculum leadership, taking a strategic view helps. This means considering the relationship among curriculum, instruction, and assessment. Unfortunately, educators often deal with these as isolated elements. Seeing them as a coordinated system probably provides much more flexibility to act. You may start on any one and develop strategies to improve all three. This will give you the room needed to move your system regardless of demands or restrictions imposed from the outside. With this more integrated view, you might, like the educators at Burruss, start to see state requirements as an interesting part of the solution, not as part of the problem.

This perspective places you as a planner in the position of selecting an appropriate point of departure—depending on your situation. Some may be able to open new schools, others may take up an opportunity brought back by a leader. In some circumstances it is best to work slowly with much community involvement in a kind of curricular metamorphosis. For school districts a good course seems to be the encouragement of local innovation that is flexibly coordinated. The good news for curriculum leaders and those who would join the adventure is that numerous access points are possible—all appear to work well. A good question to ask yourself is, What choice best fits *our* situation?

Once started, you will want to understand and protect your innovations. So far, the sites described here have been able to grow as required while maintaining their quality. But the speed and size of that growth need to be considered carefully. I worry that these schools may reach a point of overpopulation and find themselves in the ironic position of risking failure because of their strength and success.

This brings up the role of communities and their early participation in launching curriculum efforts. It was inspiring to see that the plans developed at these sites were almost always premised upon community participation. This participation differed from the concept of "community buy-in," which implies schools "selling" ideas to parents and taxpayers. Perhaps too much salesmanship in recent years has contributed to mistrust of the public schools. The schools in this study took the term *public* in *public schools* to heart. They not only included the public in their planning, they often allowed their own ideas to be reinvented by the community. All who did so felt that the new ideas were far better because of that involvement.

## Reflections on Curriculum Choices

Just as the start-up process may begin in various ways, the selection or creation of specific curriculum plans may follow several possible paths—simply because schools find themselves in remarkably varied situations. Other contributing factors include local values and priorities. But whether schools adopted, evolved, or developed their curriculum, the constant for all was long, hard work. There simply was no easy way around it.

An examination of the details of curriculum plans shows that meeting state and district mandates was possible, and no one considered these to be roadblocks. They were part of the equation and a design requirement that needed to be met.

The plans demonstrate a shared concern for learning at high levels for great numbers of students. The schools had clear standards that they labored to make more precise. Responsibility for learning was shifting to the students but with careful monitoring by faculty and administration. The curriculum plans also reflected the use of interdisciplinary projects, but not for the sake of being fashionable. Schools tended to follow Sinclair's 9th grade pattern, balancing combined disciplines with the development of skills and content knowledge in specific fields. The constant remained improved learning.

With all of their shared values, why did the sites come up with such varied curriculum choices? Their differing underlying belief systems may be one explanation. Far from being bland institutions, these schools have clear ideals that relate to four major schools of educational philosophy: essentialism, perennialism, existentialism, and progressivism. However, the individual sites cannot be neatly categorized under any one label. Even the Core Knowledge schools, whose curriculum leans heavily toward the liberal arts ideals of the perennialists, show elements of essentialism in their systematic organization and of progressivism in their use of hands-on instruction. Yet, it is important not to be fooled into thinking that any combination of philosophies will do, lest one fall victim to what might be called "a potpourri of mediocrity." The selecting and blending done by these curriculum leaders was subtle and resulted from careful deliberations.

## The Meaning of Sustaining Development over Time

The constancy with which administrators, teachers, board members, and community members treated curriculum leadership reminded me of the way one treats an important personal relationship. They did not consider the learning agenda something to be decided upon and then dispensed with in favor of more important business. Curriculum and its allied functions of instruction and assessment *were* the business of these schools because these lie at the heart of organized learning. All other activities were designed to support this core.

Although that is a noble sentiment, making such a system operational implies very serious effort by all three groups—administrators, teachers, and the community. Administrators shared three common traits that seemed to enhance continued development. First, they developed a climate that made it more likely for change to carry on. They saw to it that there was an established cycle for inventing, testing, and evaluating new ideas. They encouraged innovations, but new ideas had to find a place in the larger pattern. They also modulated speed to keep everyone excited but not overstimulated by change. This included helping to establish realistic goals. Every one of the leaders was close to the staff, parents, community, and students. They were trusted to keep the vision of their school alive.

Second, as good administrators, these leaders understood that part of their task was the creation of vital support structures. Shared governance that matured and improved over time was one crucial element at almost every site. Equally important was the habit of spending resources on exploring, sometimes by traveling to other centers of innovation. These trips were by no means vacations. Each had a specific focus to bring home vital information. The leaders valued information itself as a respected commodity, and many led efforts to share the results of extensive surveys throughout their school community. Because they had abandoned the idea of "selling" their plans, they could use this information more objectively to guide improvements. The administrators were in charge of making and maintaining positive relationships with the system beyond their school. They did not stand as gatekeepers to the outside world; rather they seemed to behave as ambassadors and advocates for their organizations. Their first inclination was to support their schools by working in positive ways with their districts and their state government. War stories were few.

Finally, administrators were thoughtful and proactive about transitions. This meant welcoming new students and their families, often acknowledging that these new members of the school community would change the organization just as they would be changed by it. The ultimate issue for the leaders, of course, was the question of their own transition. Only one of the locations had actually experienced such a transition, which went smoothly.

Compared with the role of administrators, the role of teachers in these schools was no less complex and equally demanding. The professional standard these educators set was remarkable. They embodied lifelong learning, they set very high goals and achieved many of them, they had a solid grasp of content, and they used a variety of instructional methods to bring content to life for students. While they understood their own situation well, the teachers could also describe a complete picture of their school and its relationship to curriculum leadership in general. Not surprisingly, these teachers worked long hours, sometimes alone and often in small, results-oriented teams. Individuals and teams were highly inventive and were trusted to start many good new ideas—as long as they followed the school's cycle of idea development. Teachers used shared governance as a serious opportunity to move their school forward, especially in relation to core learning activities. They were instrumental in helping shared governance evolve. Finally, teachers attended to their own professional development with gusto. They were anxious to learn about new content, methodology, and technology, but they insisted that this growth fit into the larger schoolwide plan.

Communities clearly did their part to keep schools moving forward, just as they had done in the early phases of curriculum leadership. Here again, community members played many roles, all of them important. Some community members served as goal setters and managers, helping to launch an organization and helping to govern it. Supporters and problems solvers were indispensable to their schools because they helped educators resolve vital issues in a positive fashion. Hands-on community volunteers helped to design and deliver new programs. They rounded out the circle of community support.

My colleagues in these schools reminded me repeatedly that the purpose of all this hard, focused work is the improvement of education for students. The schools measured academic success in differing ways, but students' assessments of their schools were definitely positive. They understood that their schools had a learning plan that differed from those in other places. Students who had experienced other settings felt happy to be where they were. Above all, students felt that their school treated them fairly, respected them as learners, and held high but achievable standards. Many shared the feeling that their school was an exciting place to be because of, not in spite of, an academic focus. They appreciated being treated as individuals. They felt well known by at least one adult on their campus.

## The Problem of Turbulence

With all of this careful initial planning, thoughtful development of a curriculum design, and conscientious effort to sustain curriculum leadership, it may seem unfair that these schools had to face the disturbing problem of turbulence. But, as teachers and administrators at these schools understood, the only sure way to avoid turbulence is to stay on the ground. Those who journey into the sky must be prepared. The picture of turbulence that emerges becomes less frightening when it is organized by degree of severity: light turbulence with its ongoing issues; moderate turbulence with its more specific, wavelike episodes; and severe turbulence with its lurching volatile conflicts. Whatever the level, turbulence need not cause paralysis. These school communities paid close attention to all turbulence because they knew that left alone, a small issue could explode into a crisis. Yet, they were not fixated on conflict. Neither defensive nor oblivious, they faced issues squarely, brought relevant people together, created an appropriate process, and measured results. Finally, they were intent on making sure that every interested person learned about their problem-solving work. Perhaps most impressive is the fact that these schools never gave up. Even if faced with the possible closure of their school, their courage and trust in each other remained alive.

## Unanswered Questions

As impressive as these 10 sites are, important questions still remain. One concern at several of the sites was how to make sure that their curriculum plan continues to meet the needs of learners in a swiftly changing world. A related problem involves the extent to which teachers participate in writing local curriculum plans. The study revealed a variety of possible answers but offered no easy conclusions.

Next, regardless of the curriculum direction, there is a need to better understand the role of the guiding belief systems. Do such belief systems change? How might they be combined effectively? The issue of choice is important here as well. Two of the schools allowed at least some degree of parental choice. Students elected to attend Oceana, for instance. How might increased school choice alter the kinds of curriculum leadership we might expect? A related aspect of choice came in Superintendent Bob Gilpatrick's concept of a system of schools. While this opens up an excellent opportunity for invention, including Wisconsin's first charter schools, district leaders understood the implied responsibility to create equitable standards of achievement for all students. But how can that be accomplished without impinging upon people's freedom to invent?

A final question relates to the problem of leadership transition. The founding leader was still in place in nearly every school and district described. Only Three Oaks had successfully made the transition to a new principal. These organizations are highly complex and, as we have seen, require a sophisticated, well-organized, and caring leader. The typical principal or superintendent search seems unequal to the task of replacing these leaders, because these are not generic schools. Time may well be needed to bring someone into the system and orient and train her well before the departure of the original leader. This advice sounds unconventional, but so are the schools to which it applies.

## Summing Up

Summing up is difficult because the implications of curriculum leadership are so vast. Through this study, I have had the rare privilege of sharing time with some of the best educators I have ever met. They went about their tasks without bluster, complaint, or rancor. They were, to revive an ancient term, most *workmanlike*. That is, they were dyed-in-the-wool professionals. No less inspiring were the parents and community members who spent immense amounts of time to create viable community schools. If we are going to reclaim our schools as the center of community life, it will be because of work like theirs. Finally, it is the students who make these schools come alive. Their enthusiasm and spontaneous joy in learning were obvious. Equally clear was the trust they had in their school to help them when things were not going well.

In the end, sustained curriculum leadership is not only possible, it is unavoidable if we are to face our responsibility to create a healthy democratic life at the dawn of the new millennium.

# References

Aronowitz, S., and H.A. Giroux. (1991). *Postmodern Education: Politics, Culture, and Social Criticism.* Minneapolis, Minn.: The University of Minnesota Press.

Bagley, W.C. (1926). "Supplementary Statement." In the 26th Yearbook of the National Society for the Study of Education: *The Foundations and Technique of Curriculum-Construction,* edited by G. Whipple. Bloomington, Ill.: Public School Publishing Co.

Bagley, W.C. (1964). "An Essentialist's Platform." In *American Education: An Introduction Through Readings,* edited by T. Hillway. Boston: Houghton Mifflin Co.

Camus, A. (1956). *The Rebel.* New York: Vintage Books.

Core Knowledge Foundation. (1995). *Core Knowledge Sequence: Content Guidelines for Grades K–6.* Charlottesville, Va.: author.

Dewey, J. (1916). *Democracy and Education.* New York: The Free Press.

Dewey, J., and E. Dewey. (1962). *Schools of Tomorrow.* New York: E.P. Dutton & Co., Inc.

English, F. (1988). *Curriculum Auditing.* Lancaster, Pa.: Technomic Publishing Co.

English, F., and R. Larson. (1996). *Curriculum Management for Educational and Social Service Organizations.* Springfield, Ill.: Charles C. Thomas Publishing.

Galef Institute. (1996). "Different Ways of Knowing Partnership Sites 1995–1996." Los Angeles: Galef Institute.

Glickman, C. (1985). *Supervision of Instruction.* Boston: Allyn and Bacon, Inc.

Gross, S.J. (April 1996). "Creating a Learner's Bill of Rights: Vermont's Town Meeting Approach." *Educational Leadership* 53, 7: 50–53.

Heschel, A.J. (1955). *God in Search of Man.* New York: Farrar, Straus, and Giroux.

Hirsch, E.D. (1988). *Cultural Literacy: What Every American Needs to Know*. New York: Vintage Books.

Hudson Institute. (April 1995). *The Modern Red Schoolhouse: Primary, Intermediate, and Upper Levels Standards*. Indianapolis, Ind.: Hudson Institute.

Hudson Institute. (1995). *The Case for a Modern Red Schoolhouse*. Indianapolis, Ind.: Hudson Institute.

Hutchins, R.M. (1964). "A Liberal Education." In *American Education: An Introduction Through Readings*, edited by T. Hillway. Boston: Houghton Mifflin Co.

Kentucky Department of Education. (1994). *Kentucky's Learning Goals and Academic Expectations*. Frankfort, Ky.: Kentucky Department of Education.

Kern, S. (1986). *The Culture of Time and Space, 1880–1918*. Cambridge, Mass.: Harvard University Press.

Kliebard, H.M. (1986). *The Struggle for the American Curriculum*, 1893–1958. Boston: Routledge and Kegan Paul.

Leithwood, K.A. (February 1992). "The Move Towards Transformational Leadership." *Educational Leadership* 49, 5: 8-12.

Lieberman, A. (1995). *The Work of Restructuring Schools: Building from the Ground Up*. New York: Teachers College Press.

Maslow, A. (1954). *Motivation and Personality*. New York: Harper & Row.

Ontario Ministry for Education and Training. (1993). *The Common Curriculum Grades 1-9*. Toronto, Canada: Ontario Ministry for Education and Training.

Parkhurst, H. (1922). *Education on the Dalton Plan*. New York: E.P. Dutton & Co.

Rugg, H. (1926). *The Foundations and Technique of Curriculum Construction*. Bloomington, Ill.: Public School Publishing Company.

Taba, H. (1962). *Curriculum Development: Theory and Practice*. New York: Harcourt, Brace and World, Inc.

U.S. Bureau of Education. (1893). *Report of the Committee of Ten on Secondary Education*. Washington, D.C.: Government Printing Office.

Weston, S.P., and R. Harmon. (1995). *Nuts and Bolts*. Danville, Ky.: Kentucky Association of Schools Councils.

Whitehead, A.N. (1929). "The Aims of Education." In *The Aims of Education and Other Essays*. New York: The Free Press.

# About the Author

S teven J. Gross is Associate Professor of Education at Trinity College of Vermont, where his teaching and research focus on curriculum leadership, instruction, and the appropriate uses of technology in schools. Previously, Gross served as Chief of Curriculum and Instruction at the Vermont Department of Education where he led the effort to write the Vermont Common Core of Learning, known for its inclusion of thousands of local residents. In addition, he has held the post of Executive Director of the China Project Consortium, working with hundreds of teachers and administrators to increase their ability to teach about and travel to China.

Gross has written for publications including *Educational Leadership* and *The Executive Educator* and has presented at regional, national, and international conferences. He lives among the Green Mountains with his wife, two children, and cat Victoria. This is his first book.

Gross can be reached at Trinity College of Vermont, 208 Colchester Avenue, Burlington, Vermont 05401 USA; phone: 802-658-0337; e-mail: gross@charity.trinityvt.edu